Owls Coloring Book for kids

THIS BOOK BELONGS TO

_____

_____

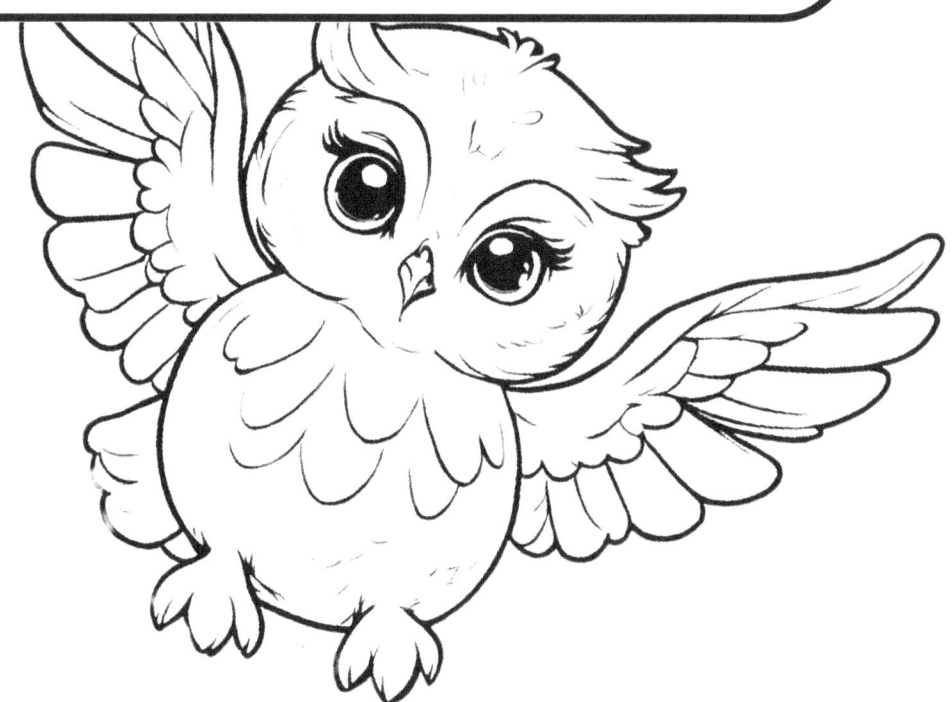

COLOR TEST PAGE

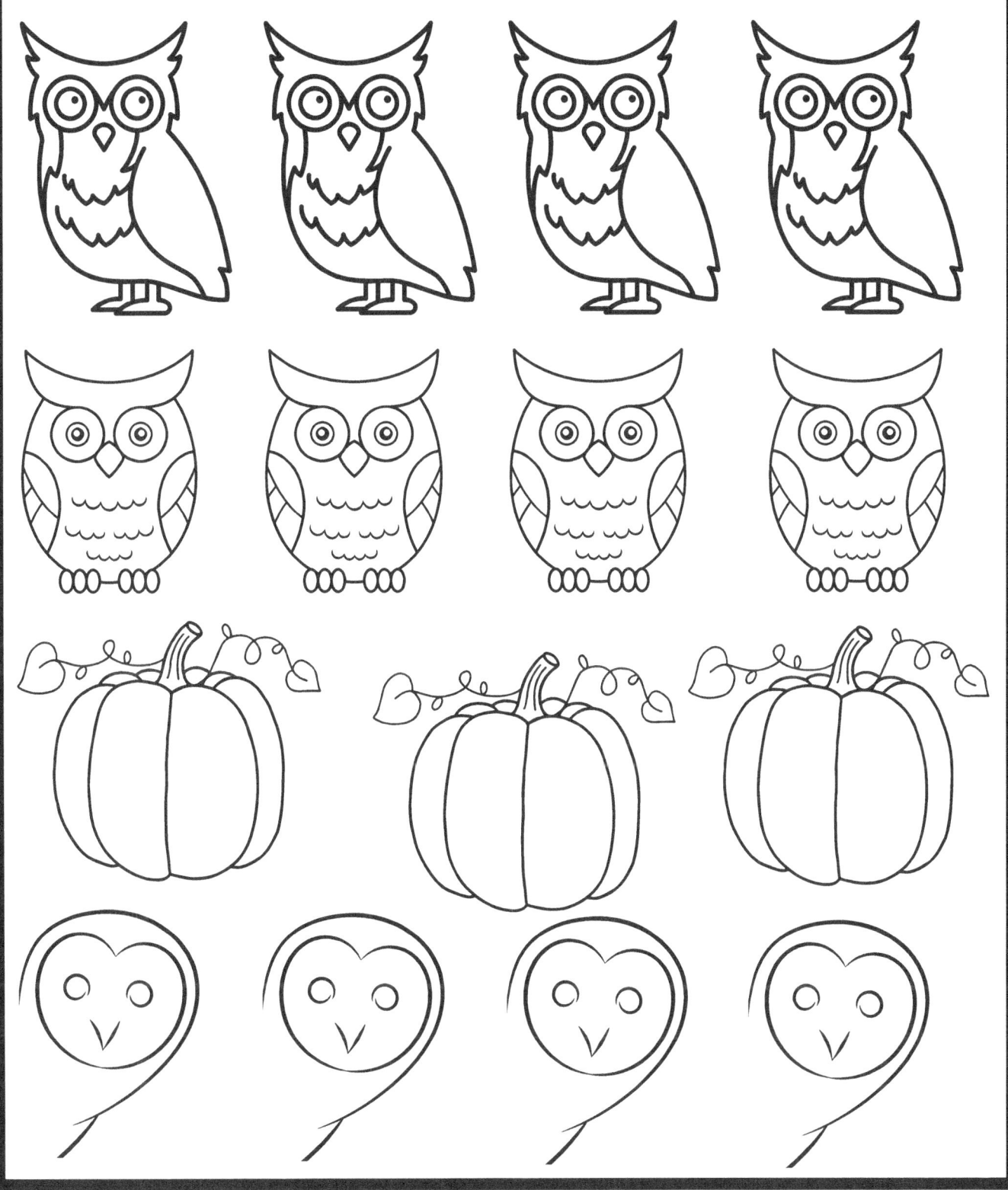

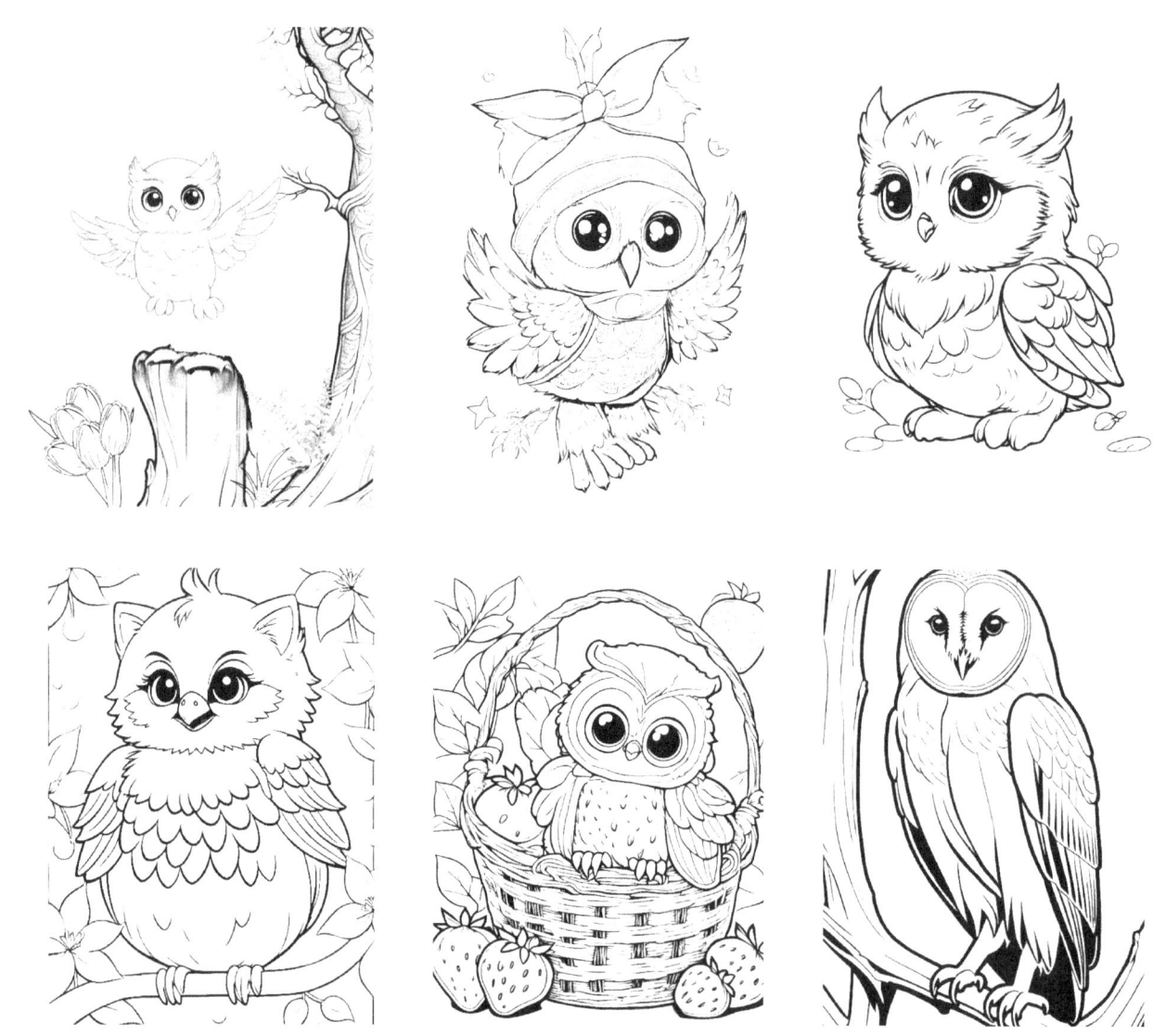

Beautiful illustrations ,
Best For all skill levels
Perfect gift for everyone for every occasion.
Single-sided Pages. Separately printed sheets to prevent bleed, 100 pages
high-quality paper,
 Dimensions:8.5*11 inches

ISBN: 9798863953458

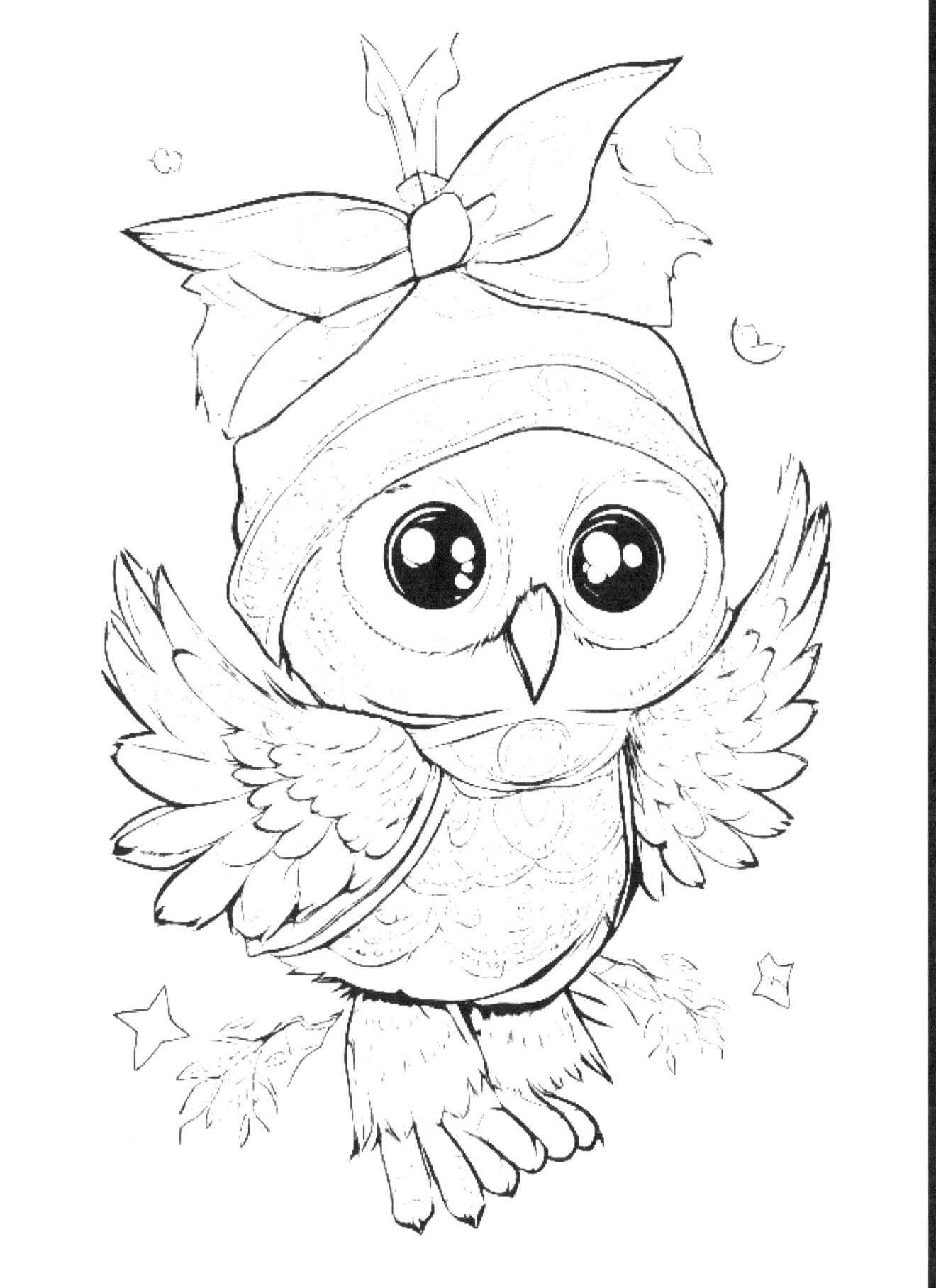

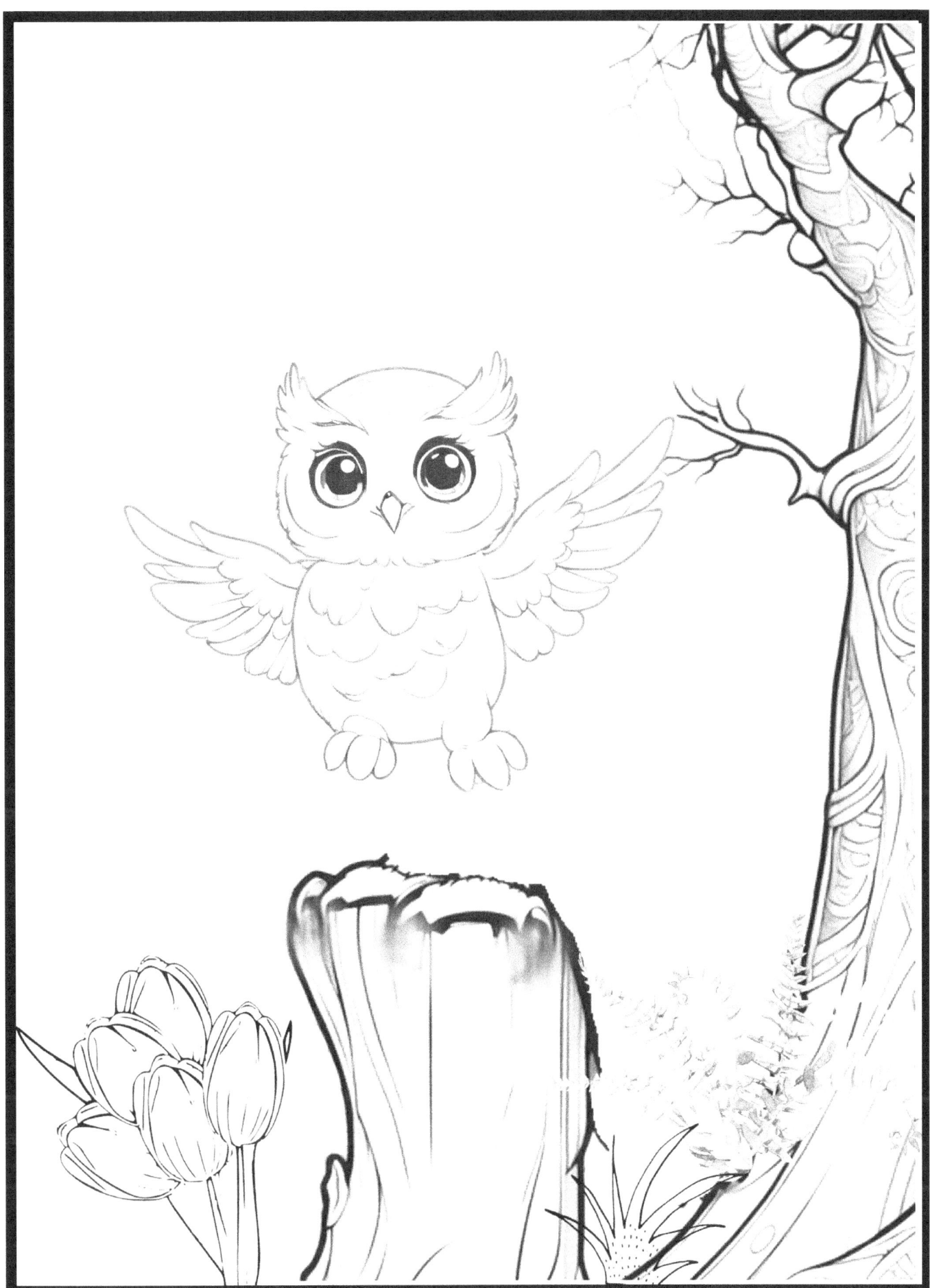

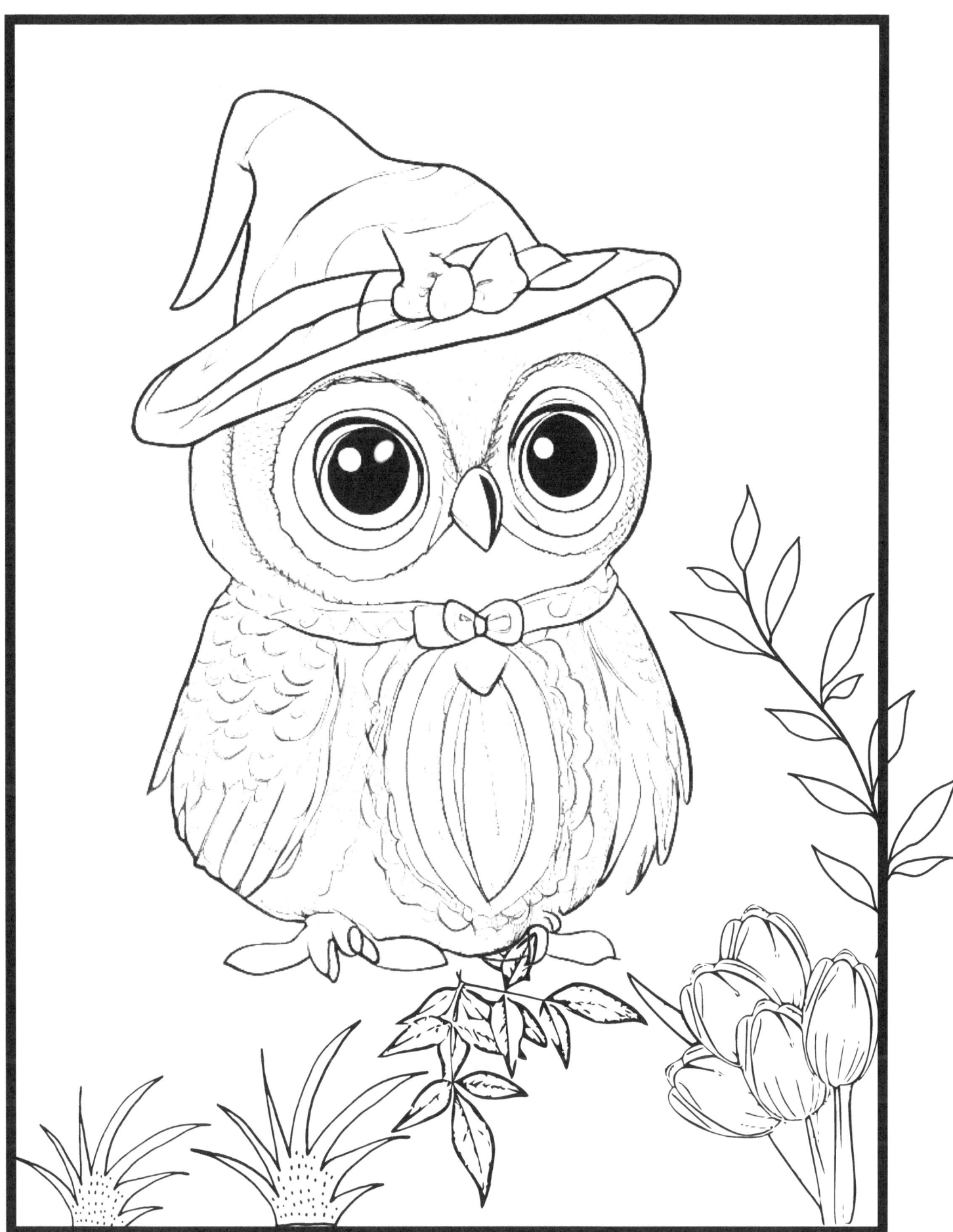

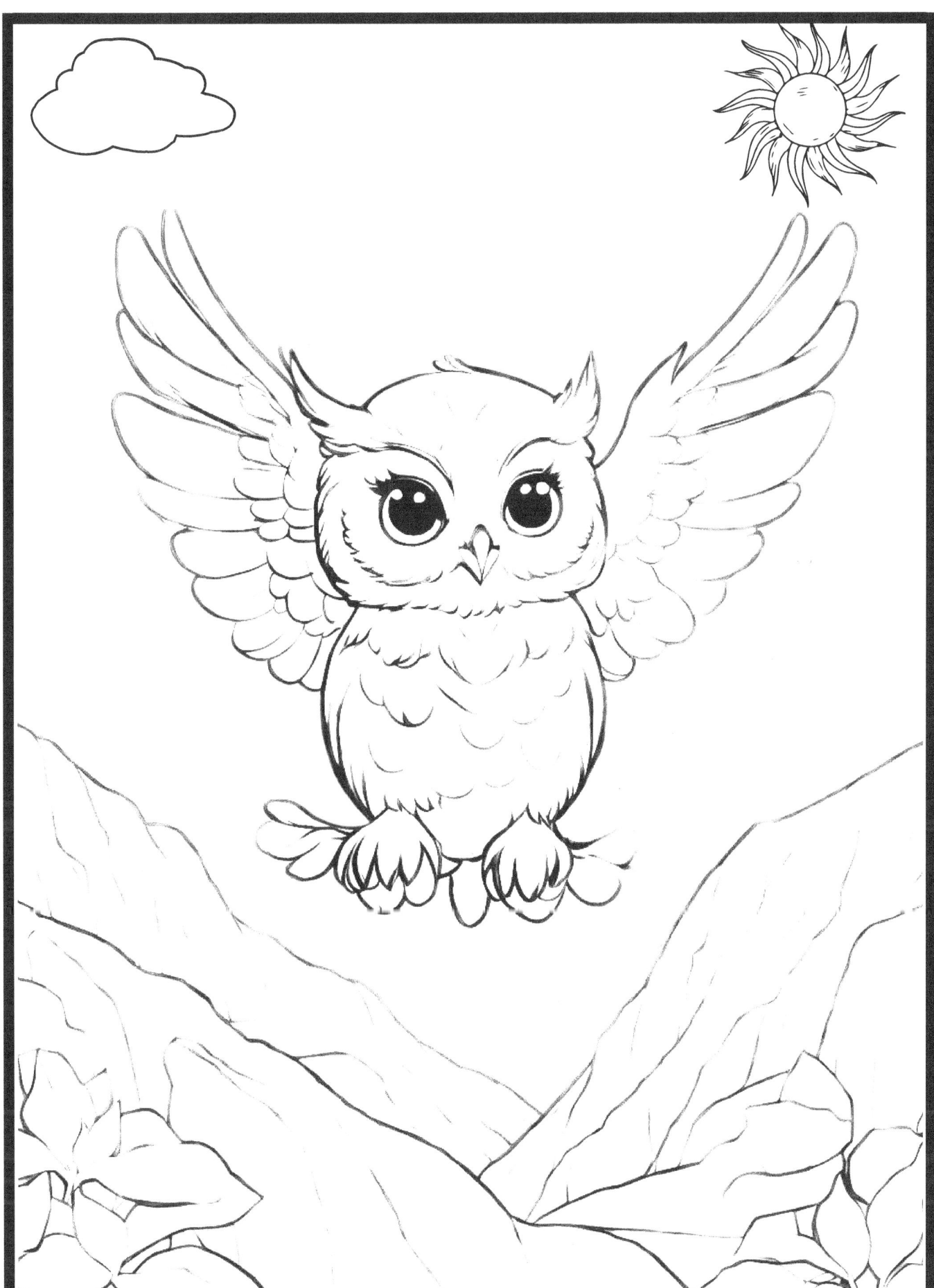

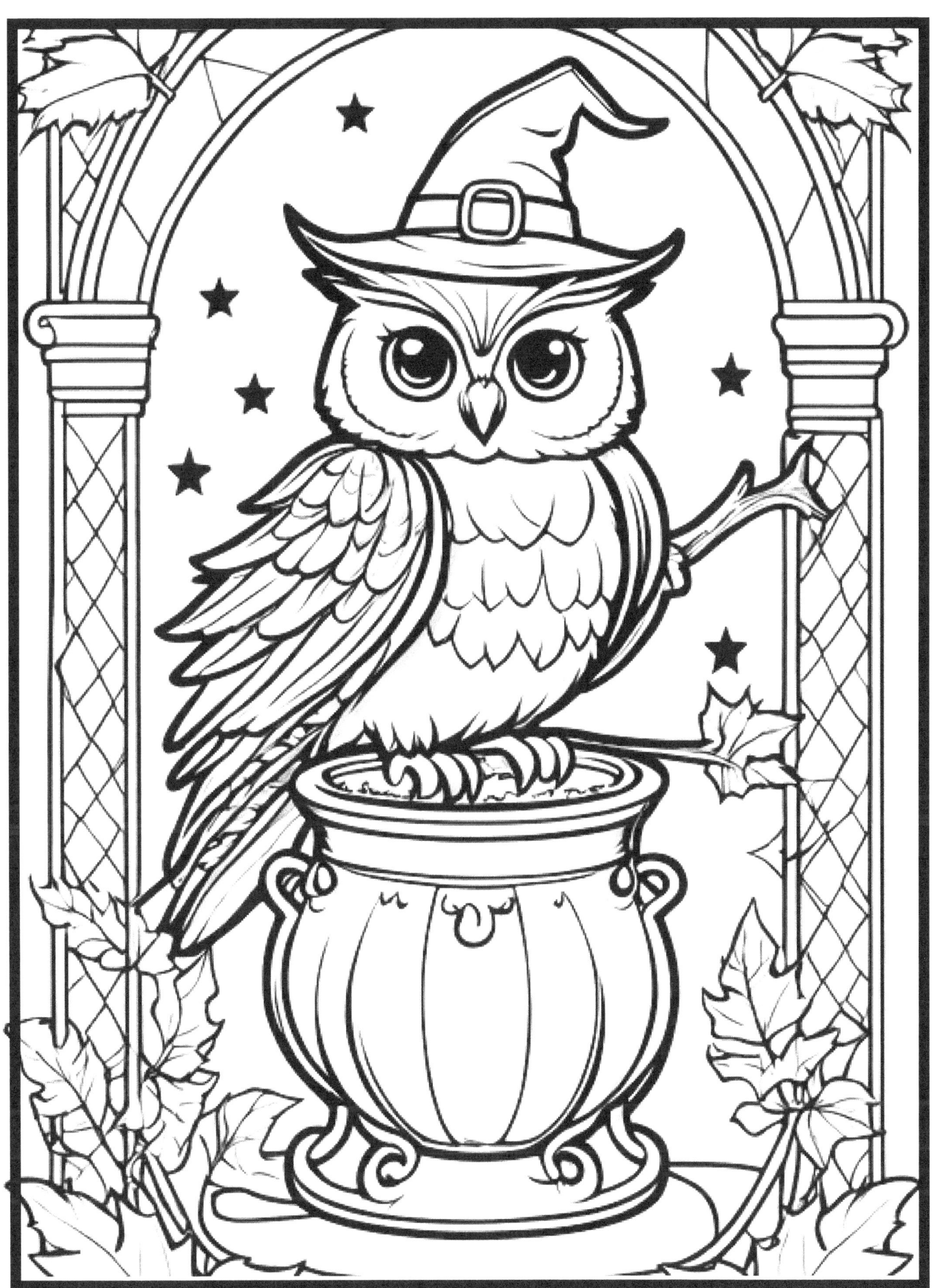

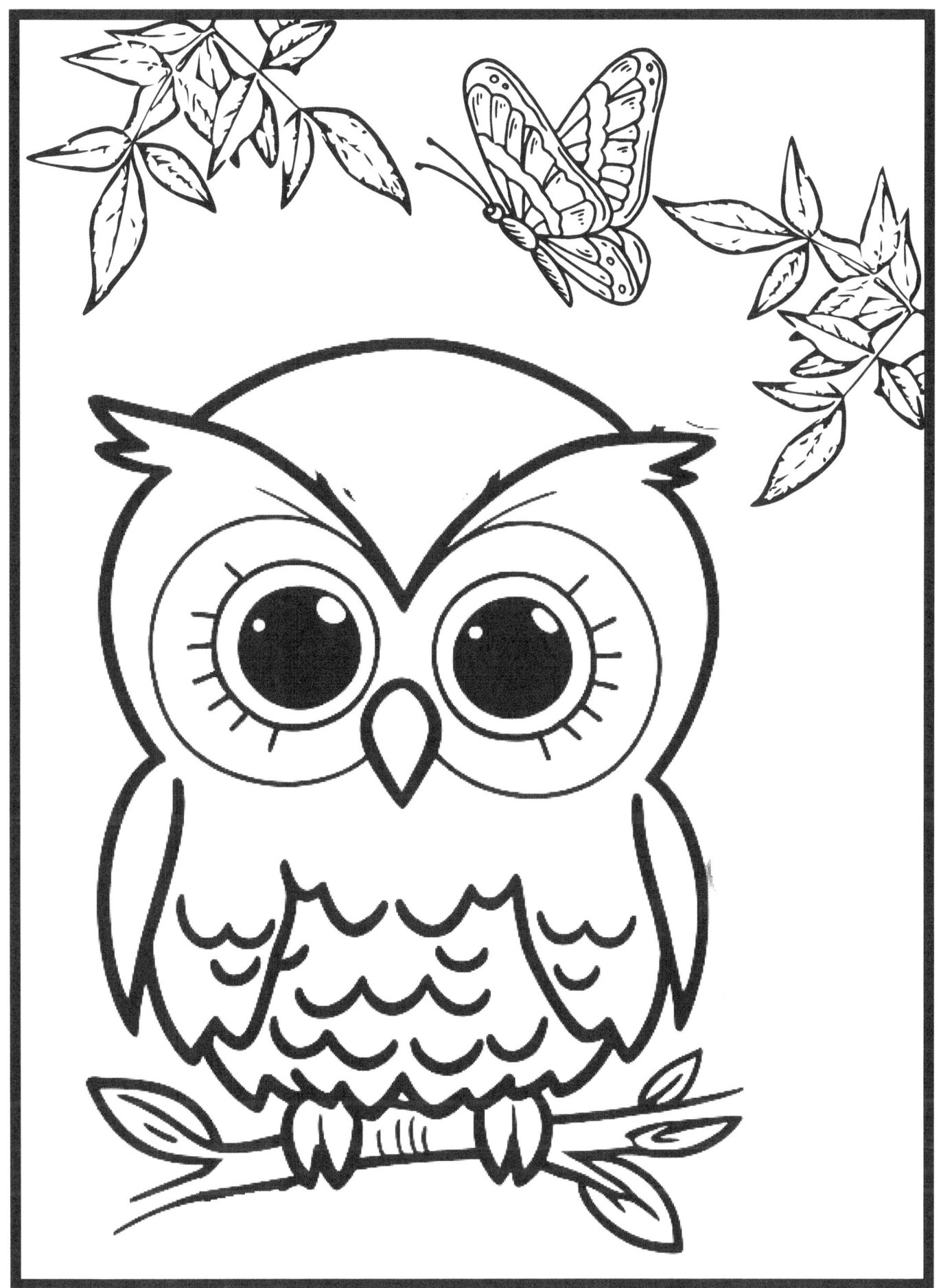

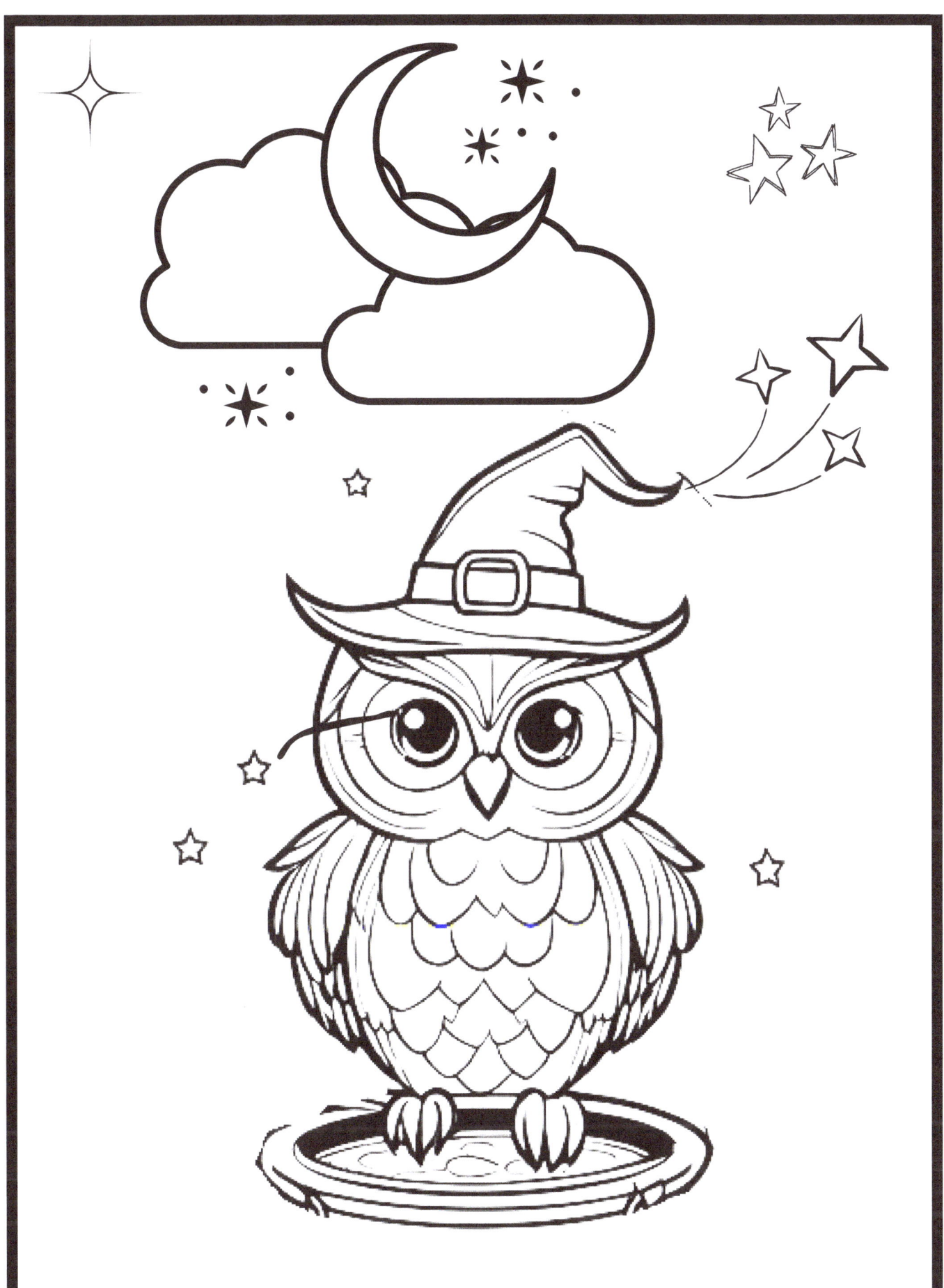

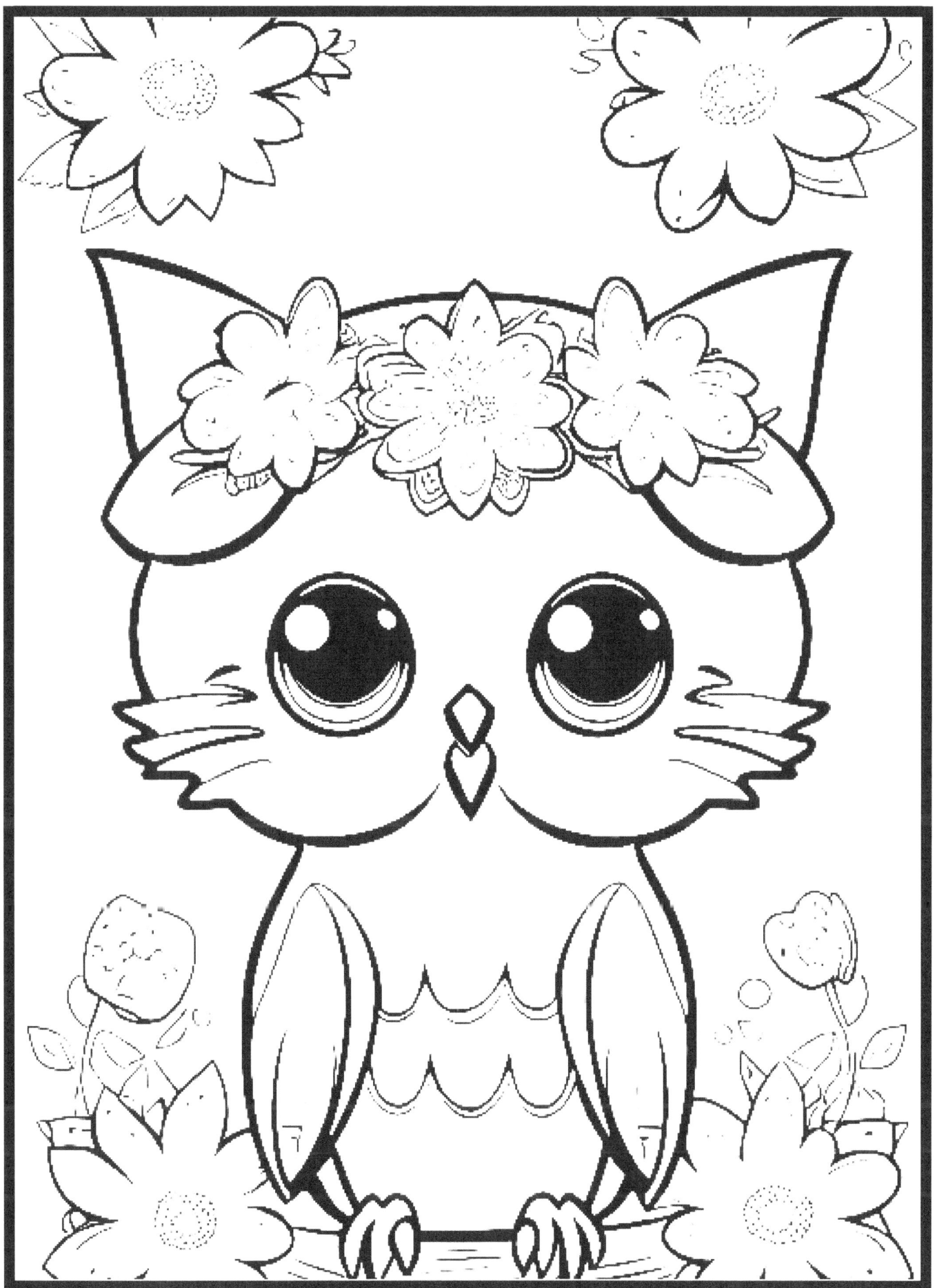

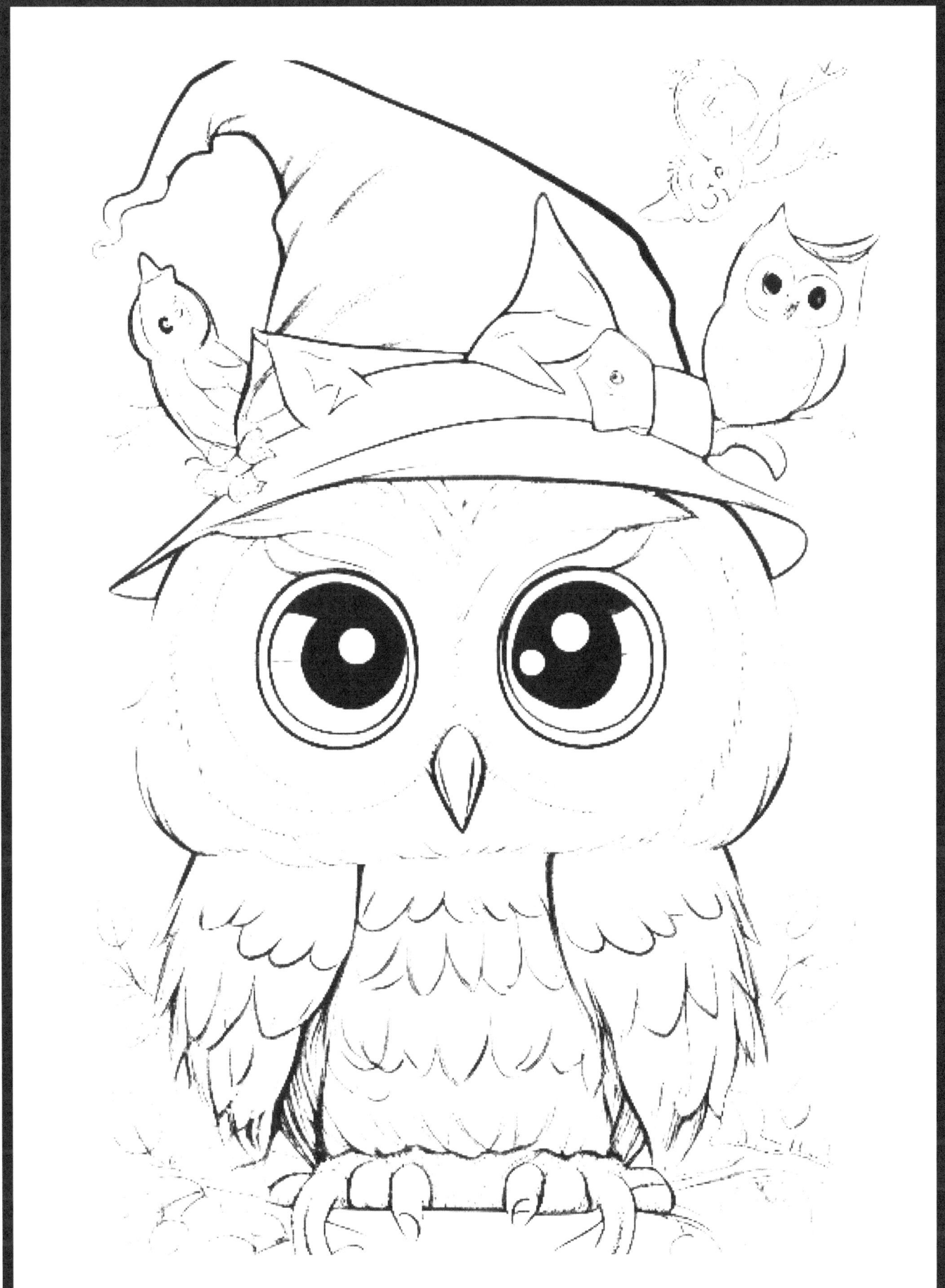

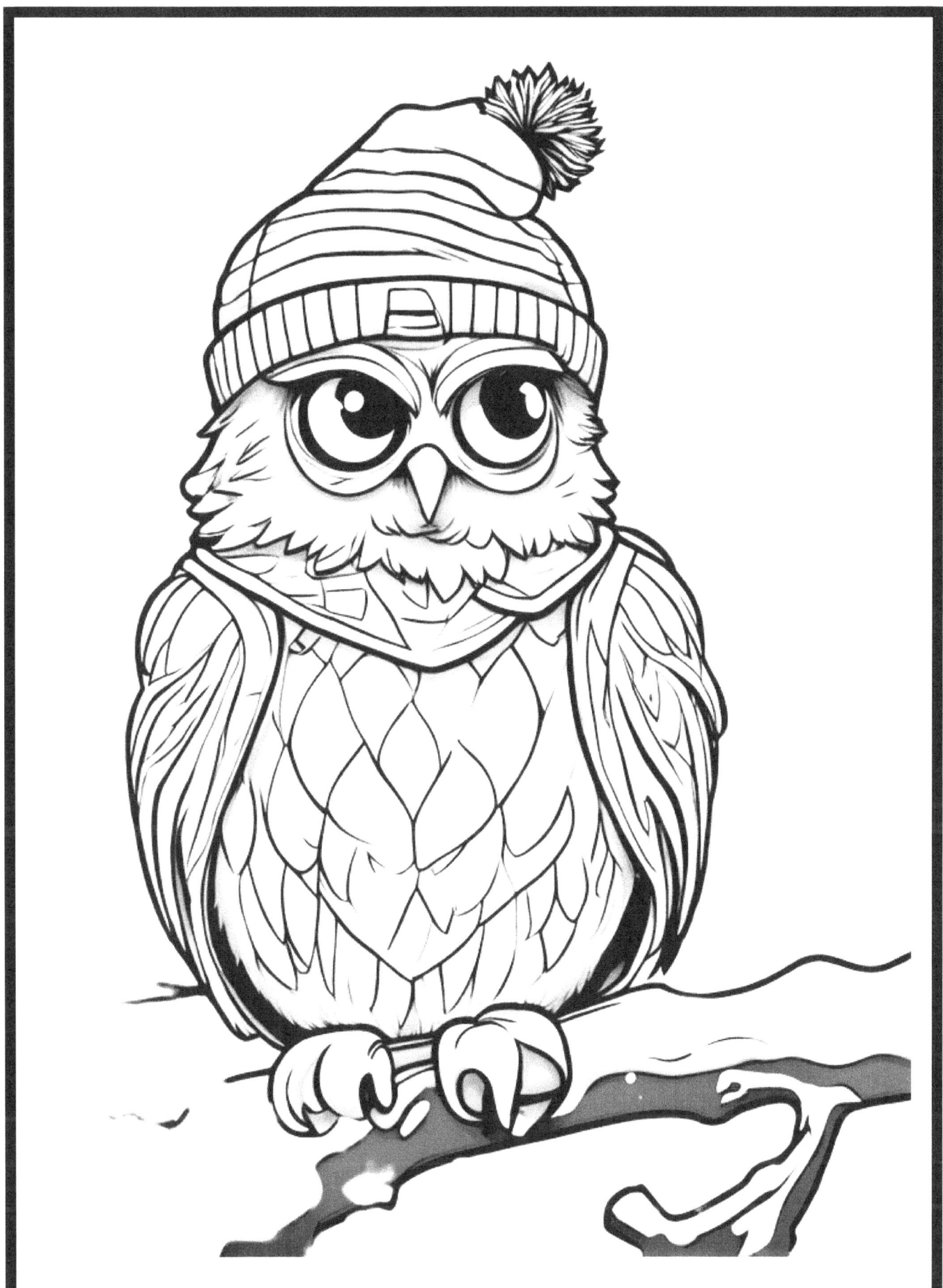

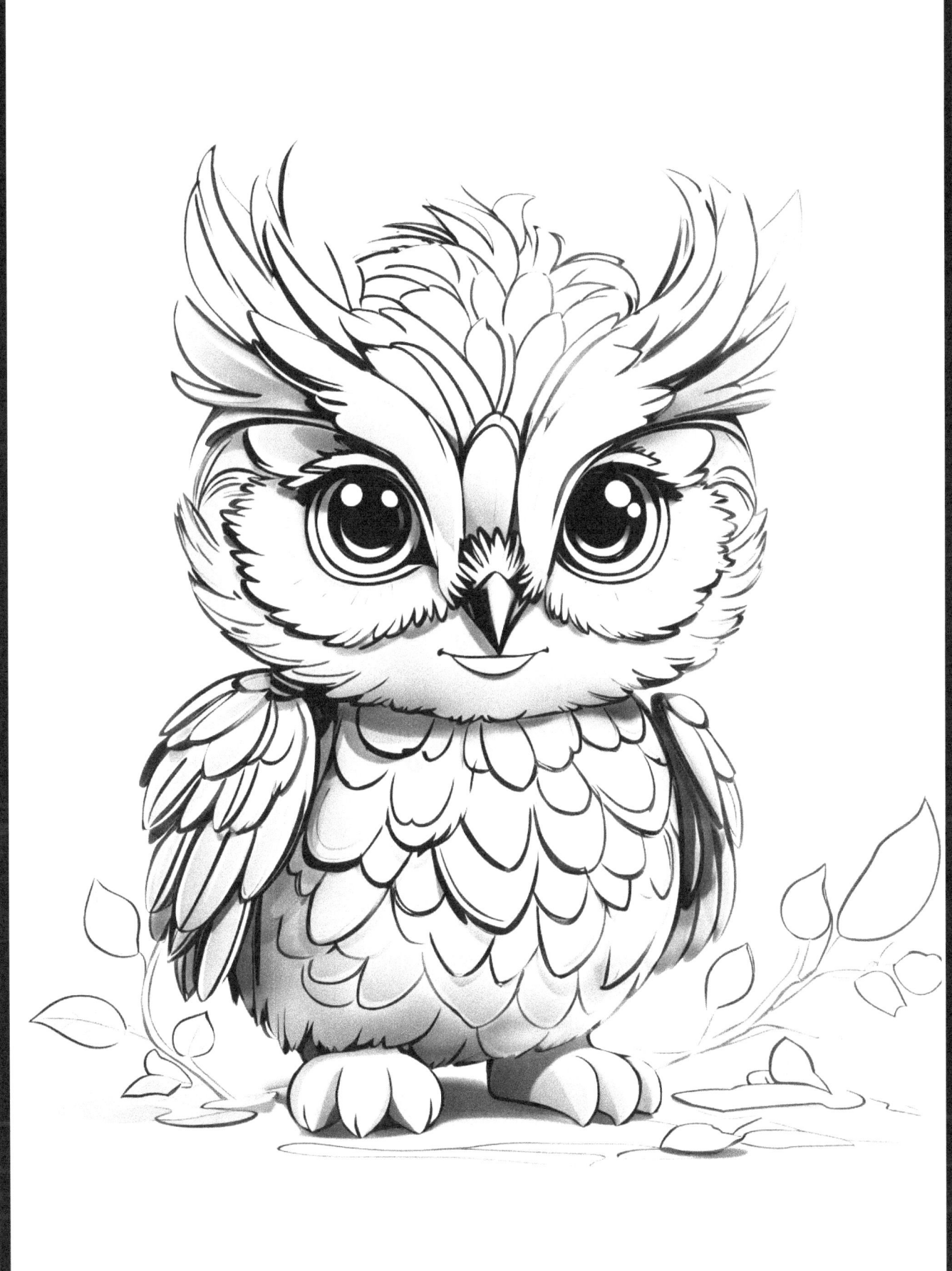

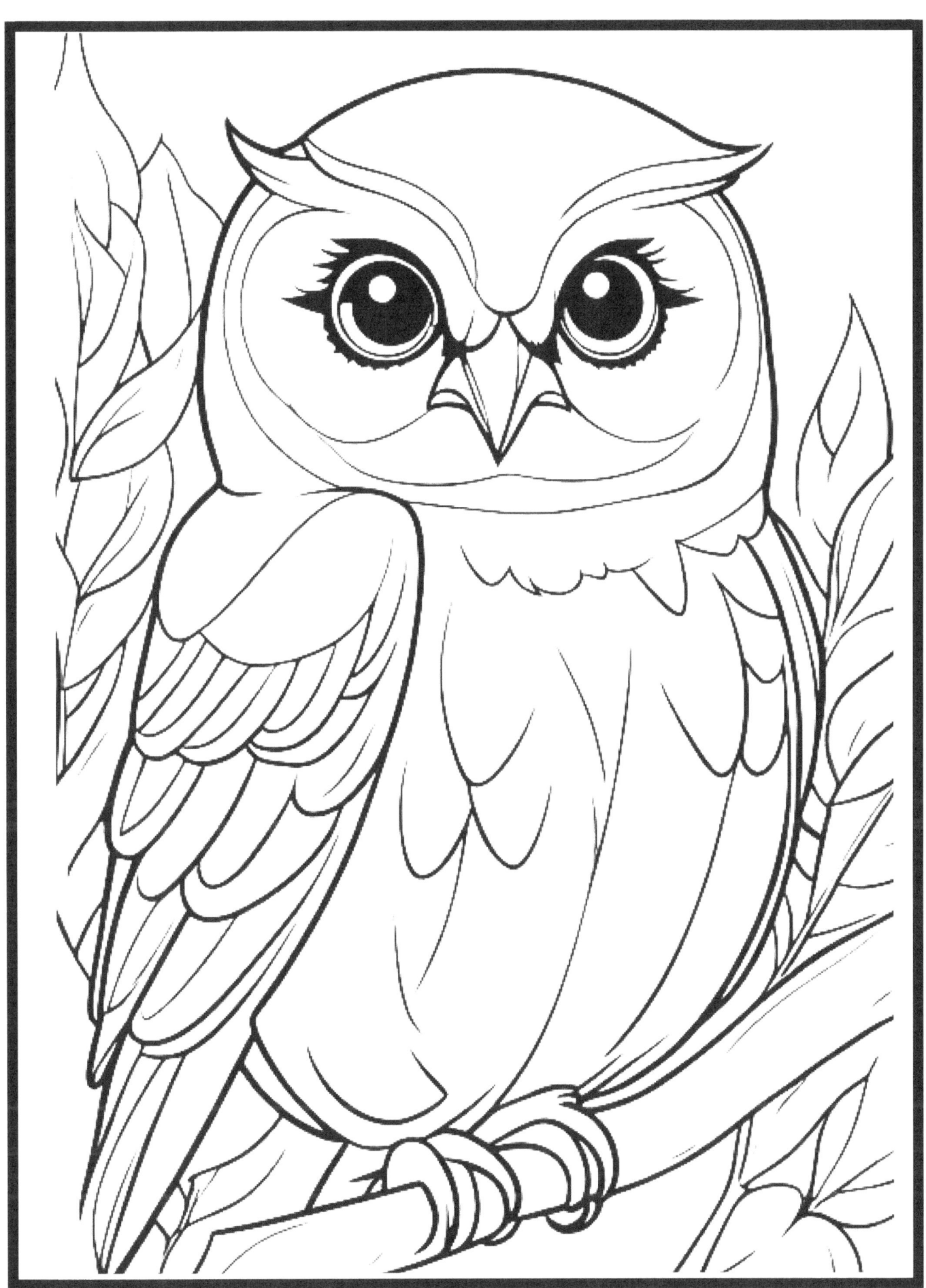

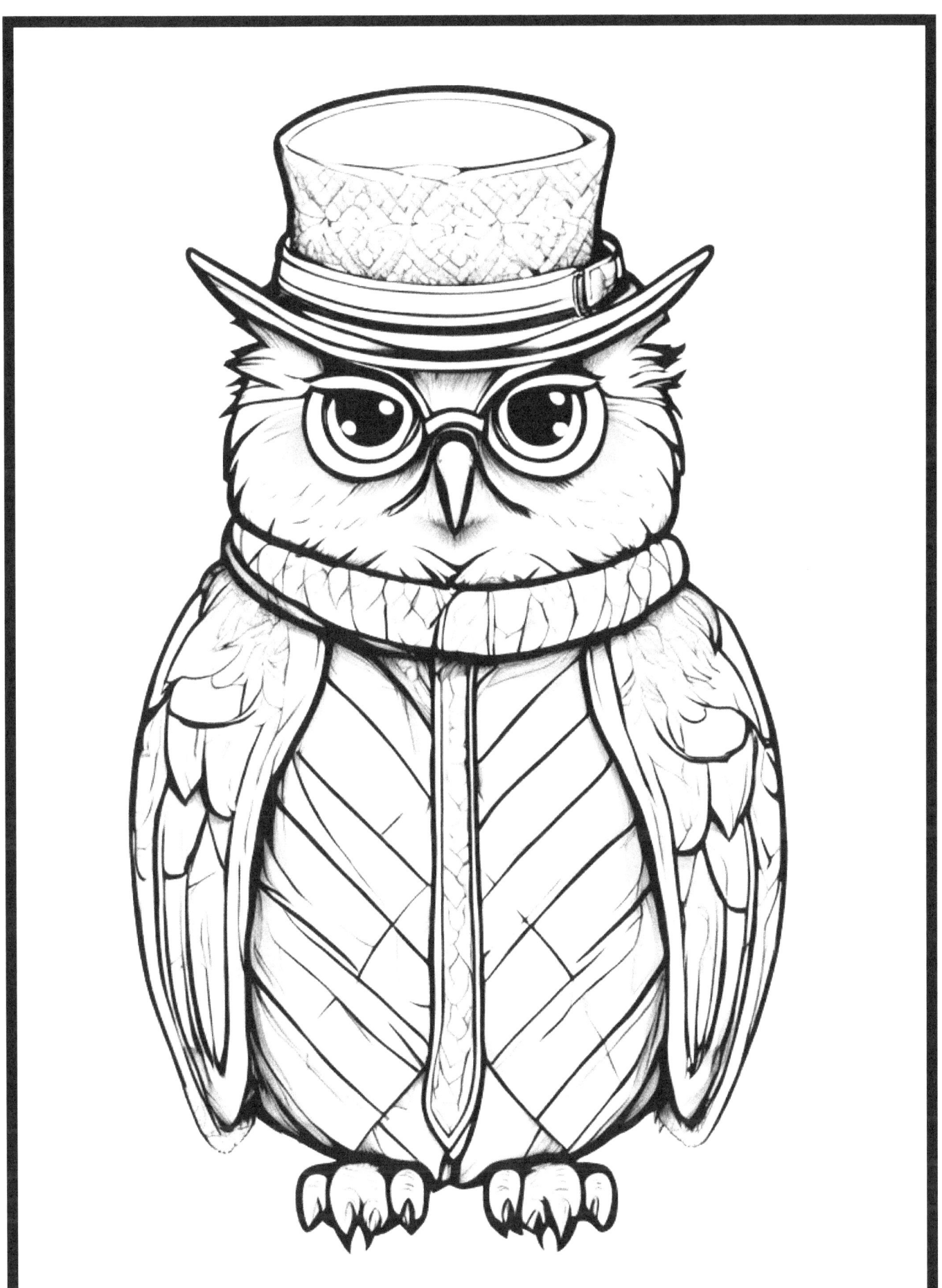

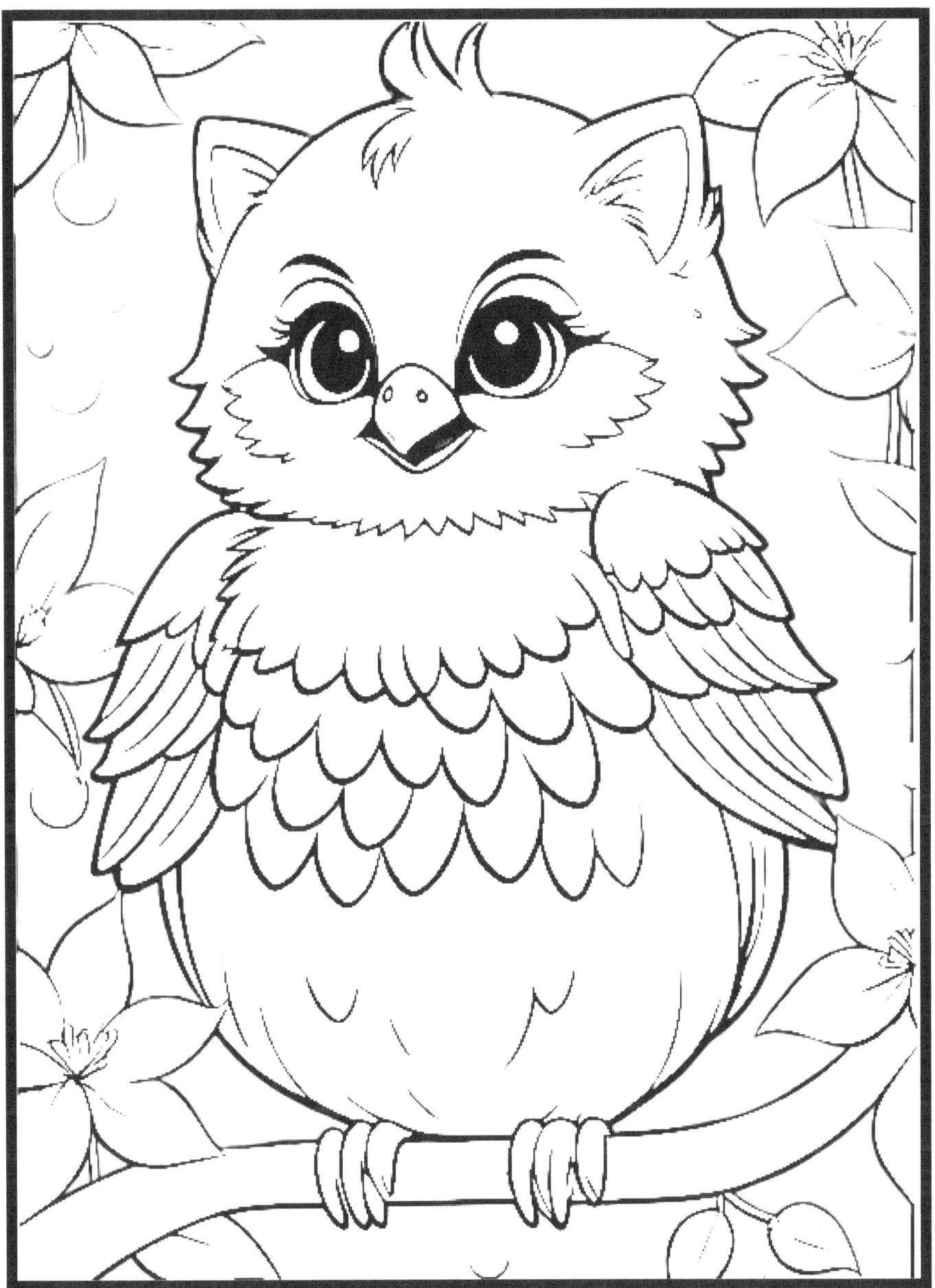

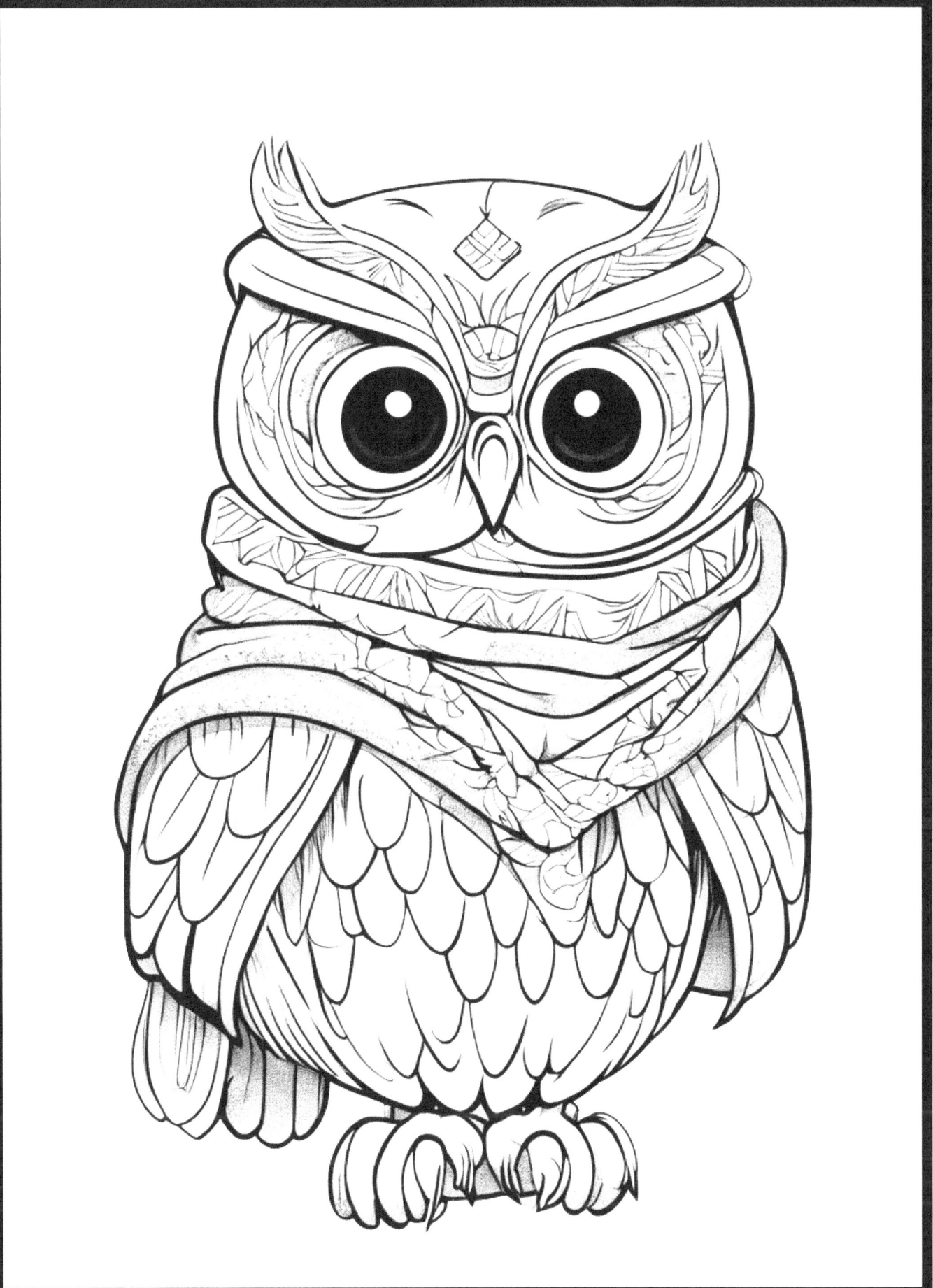

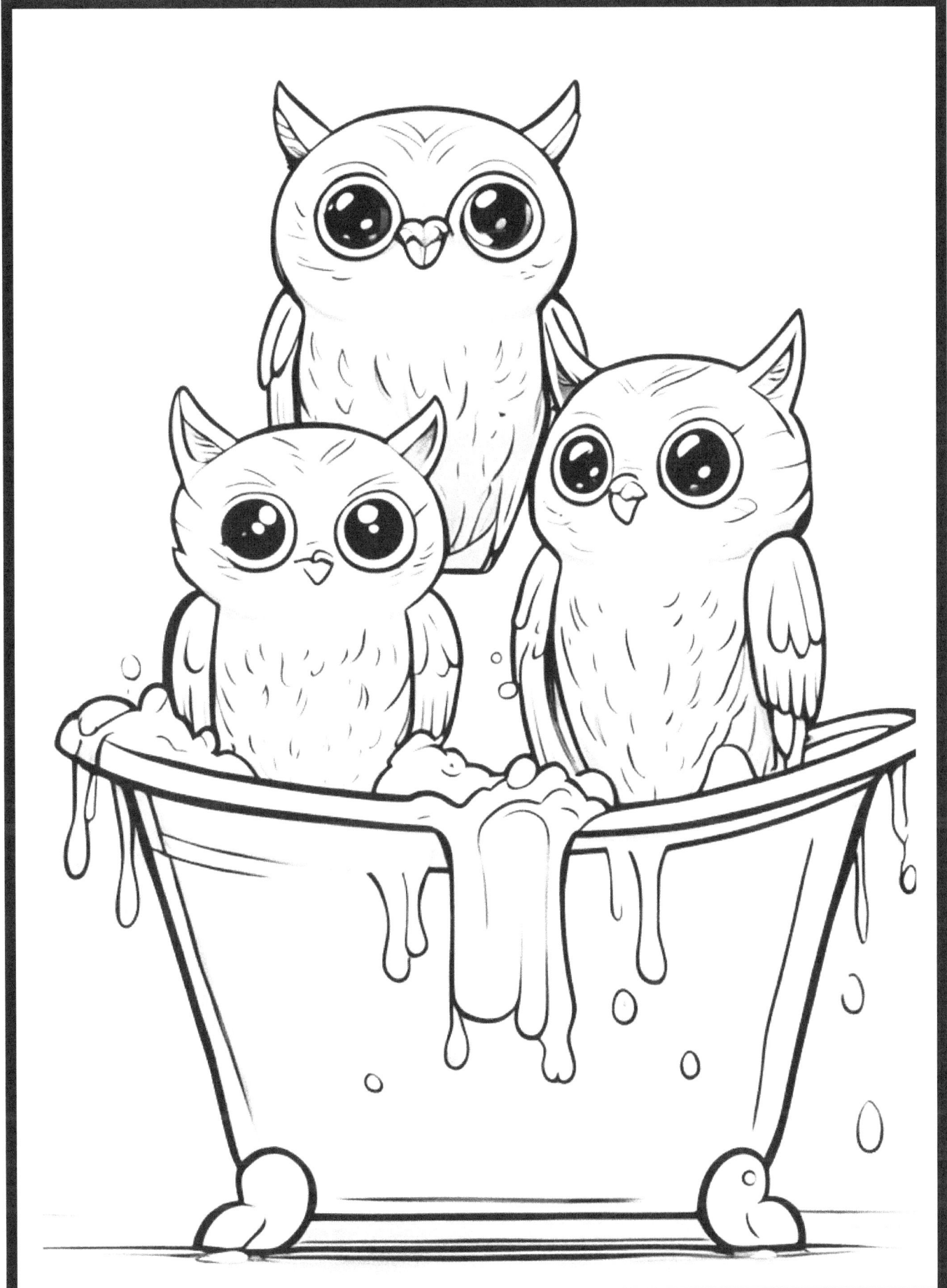

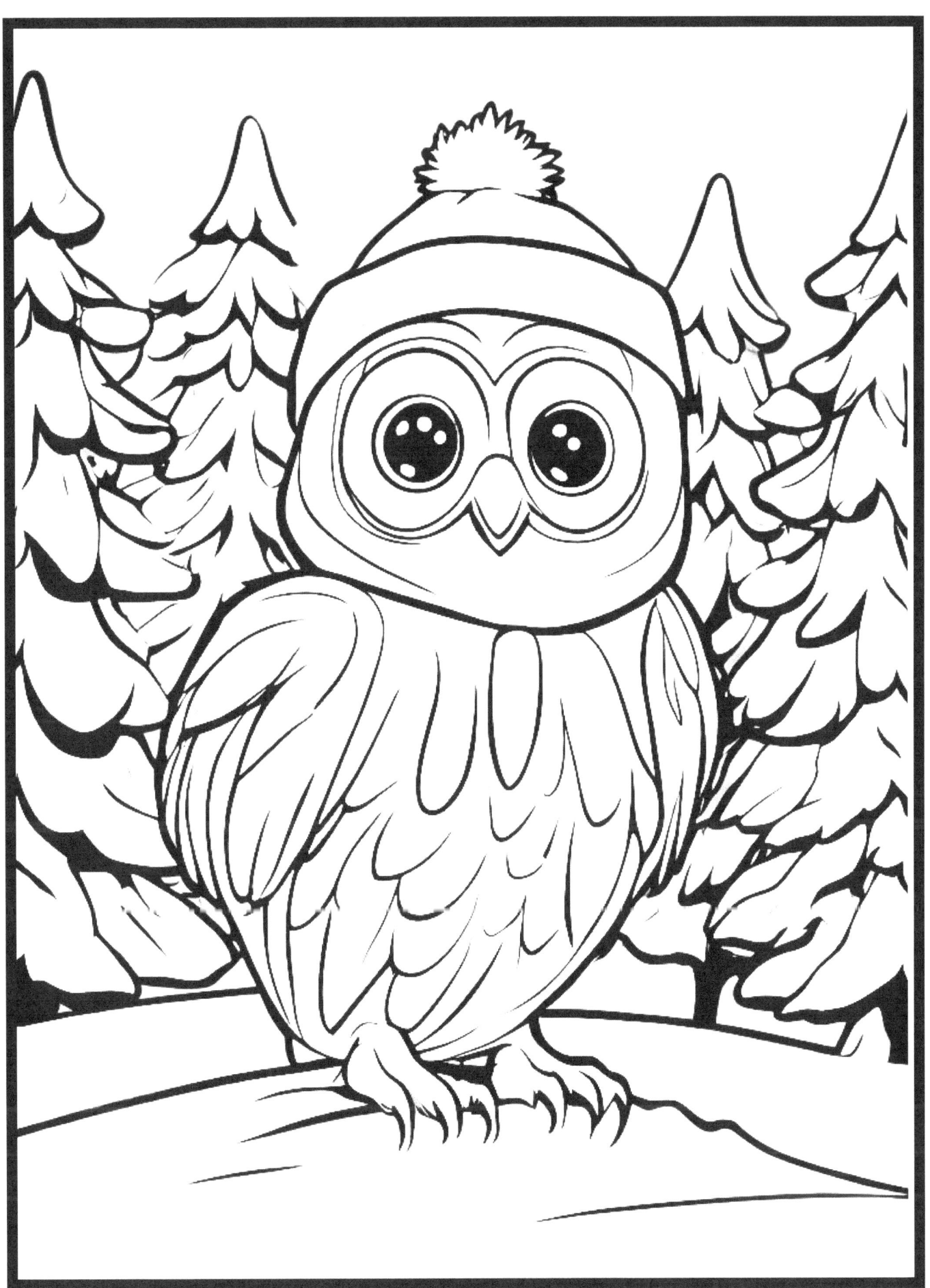

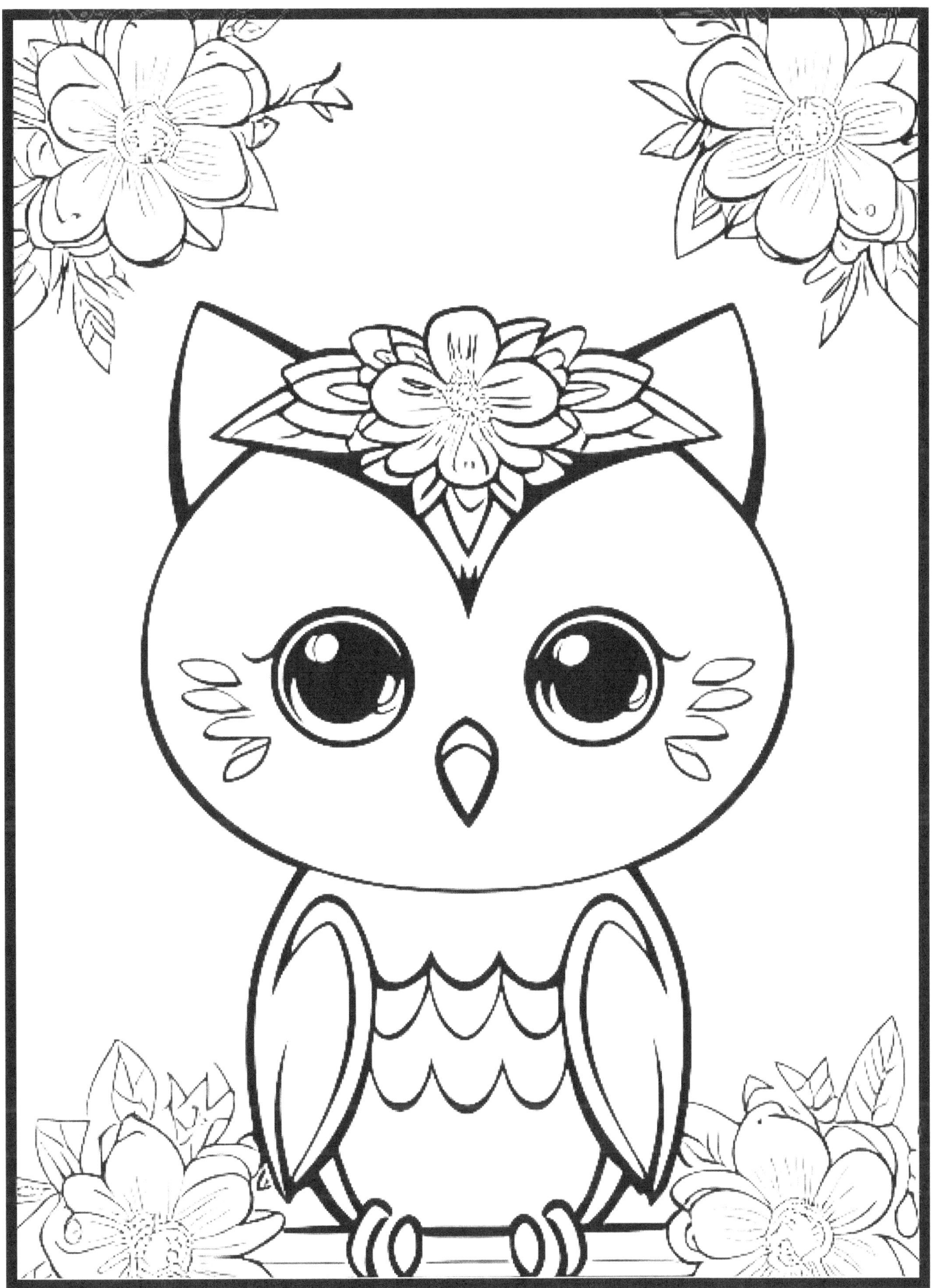

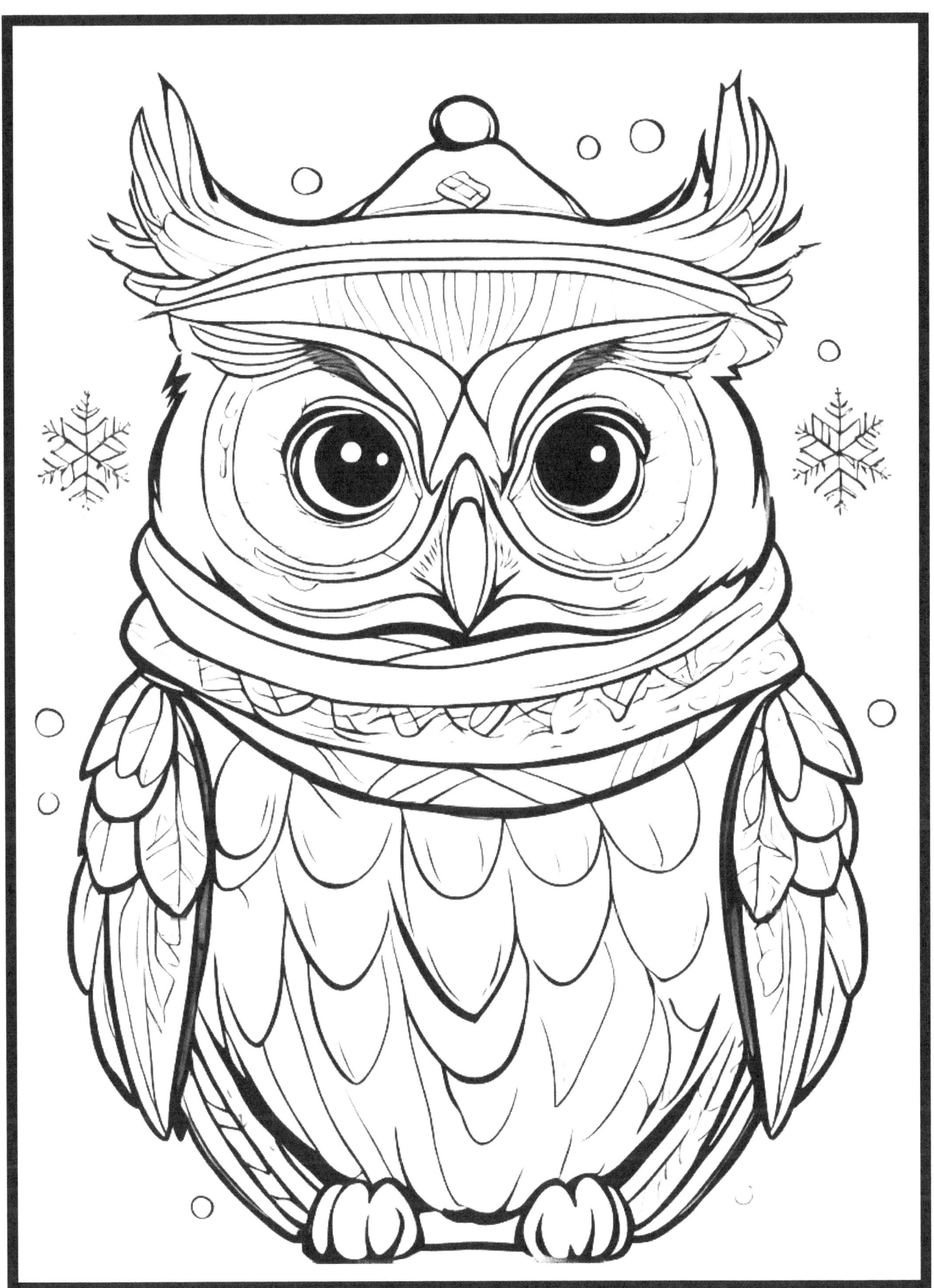

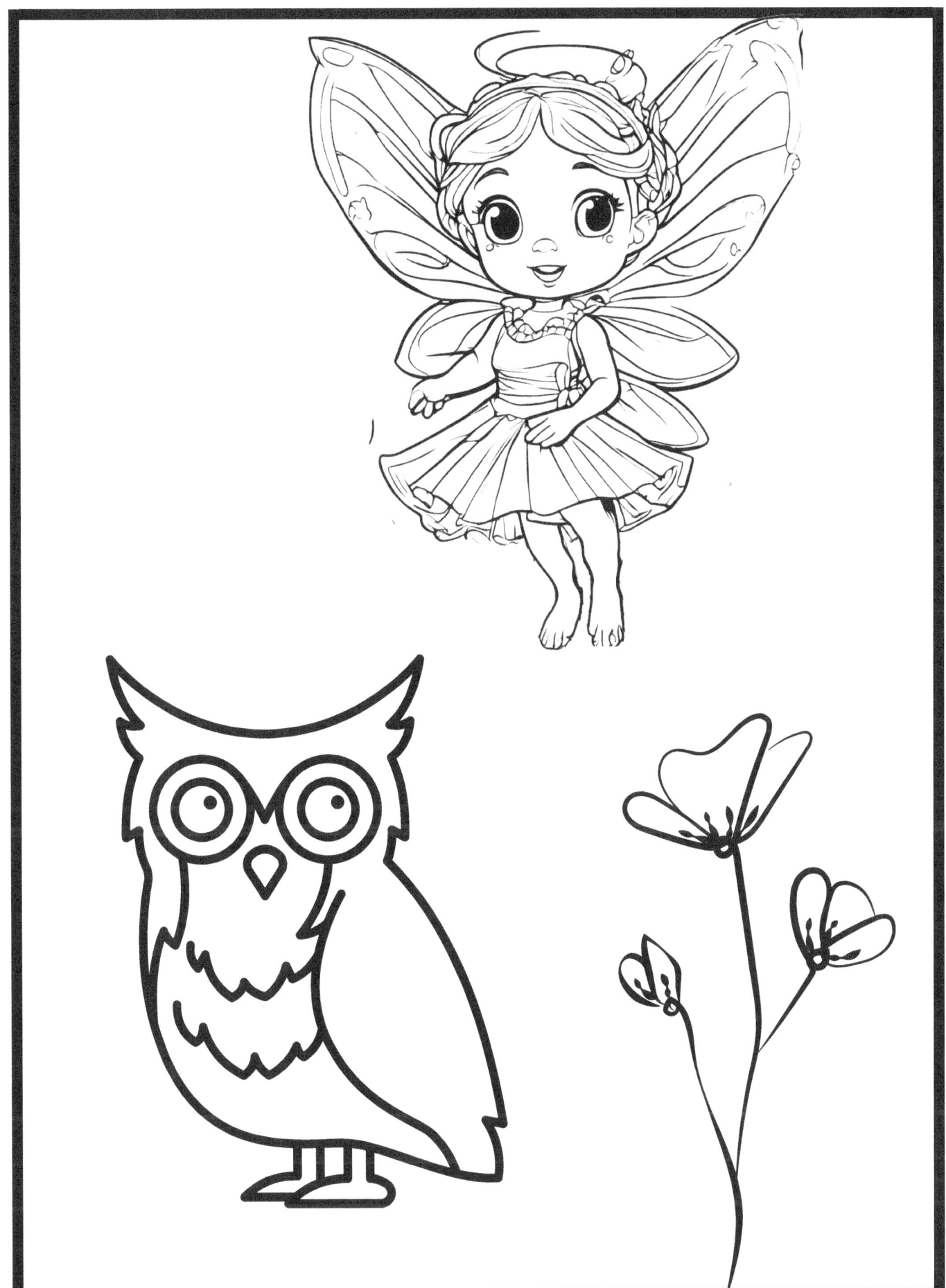

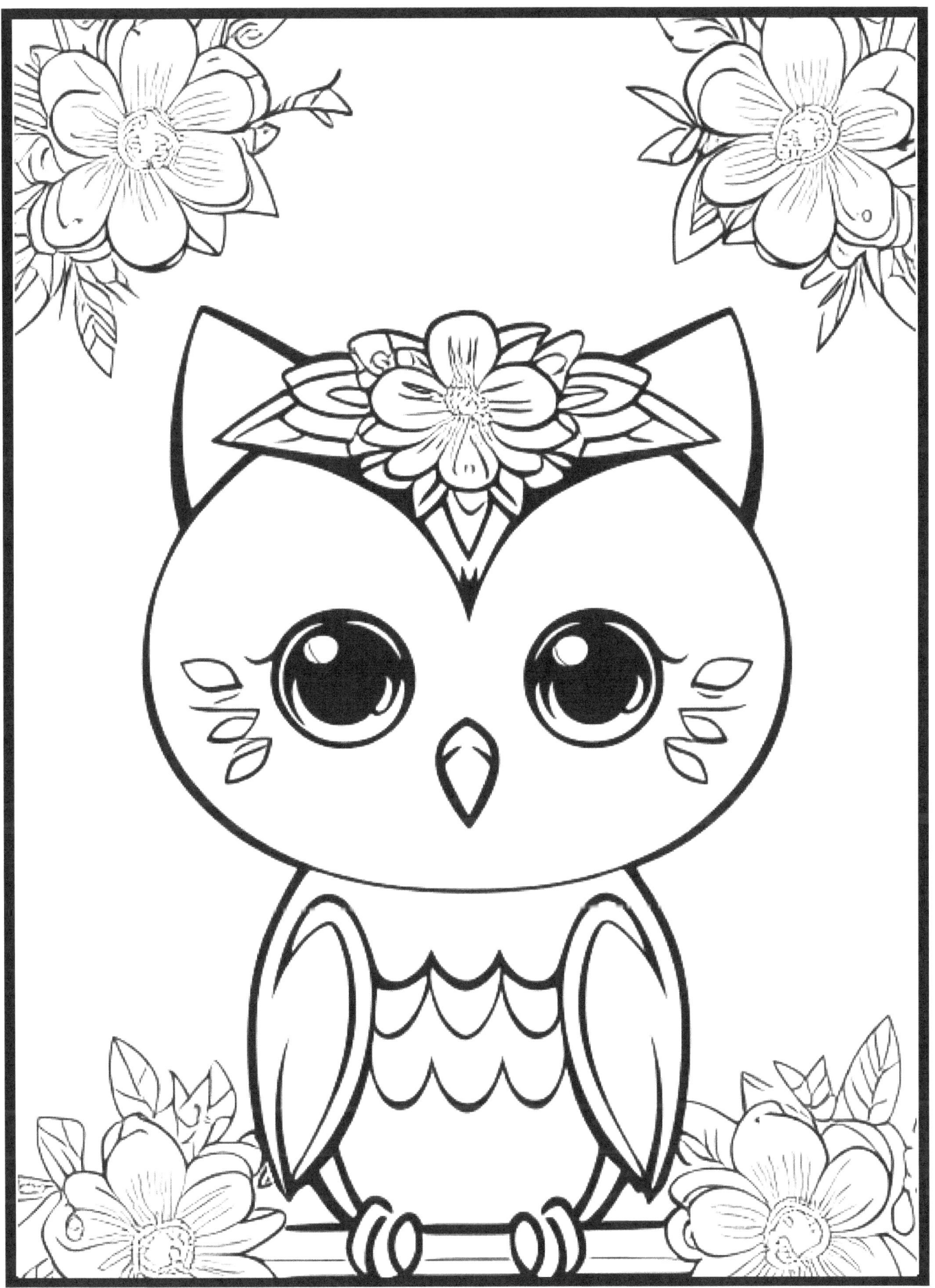

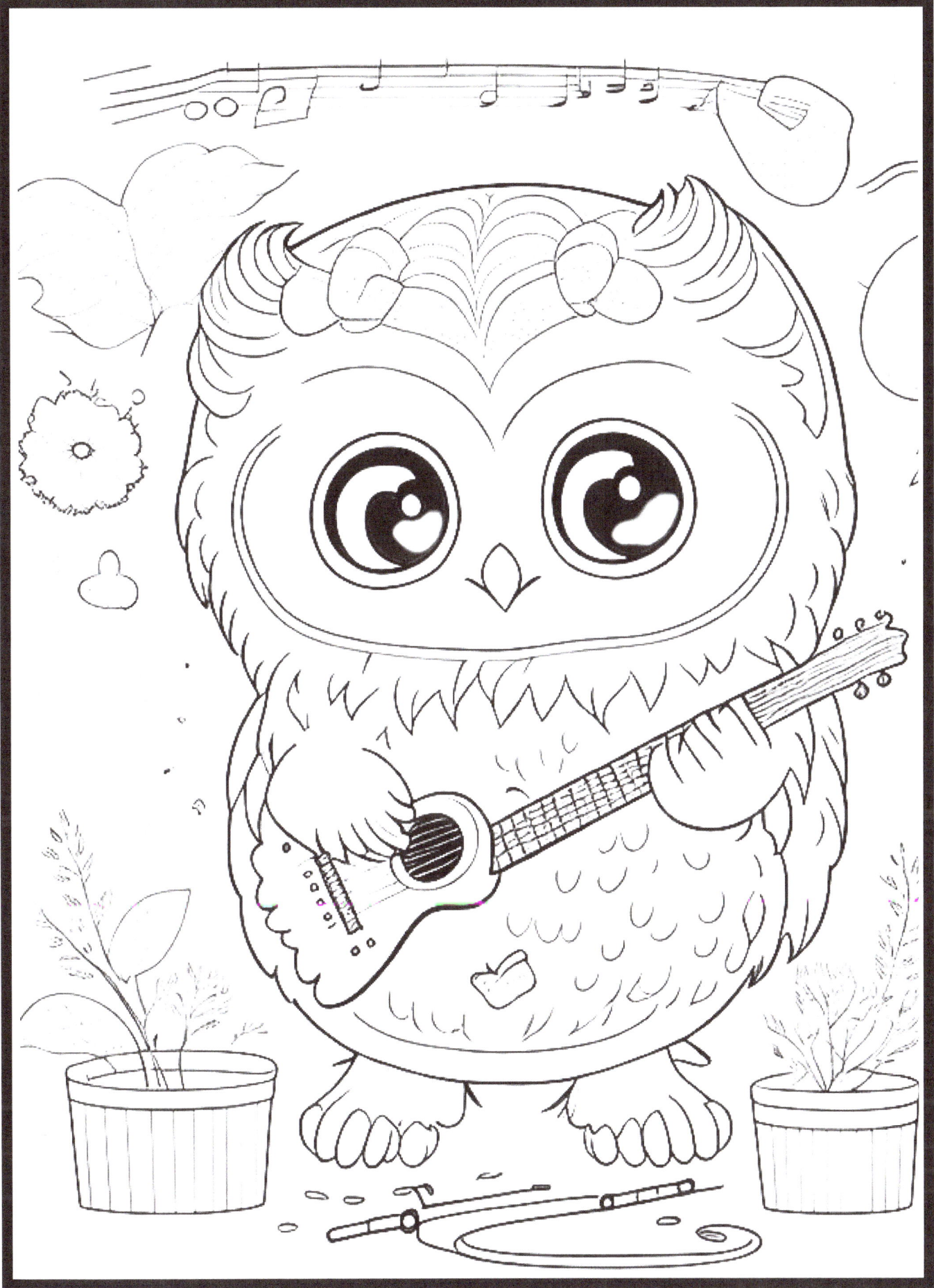

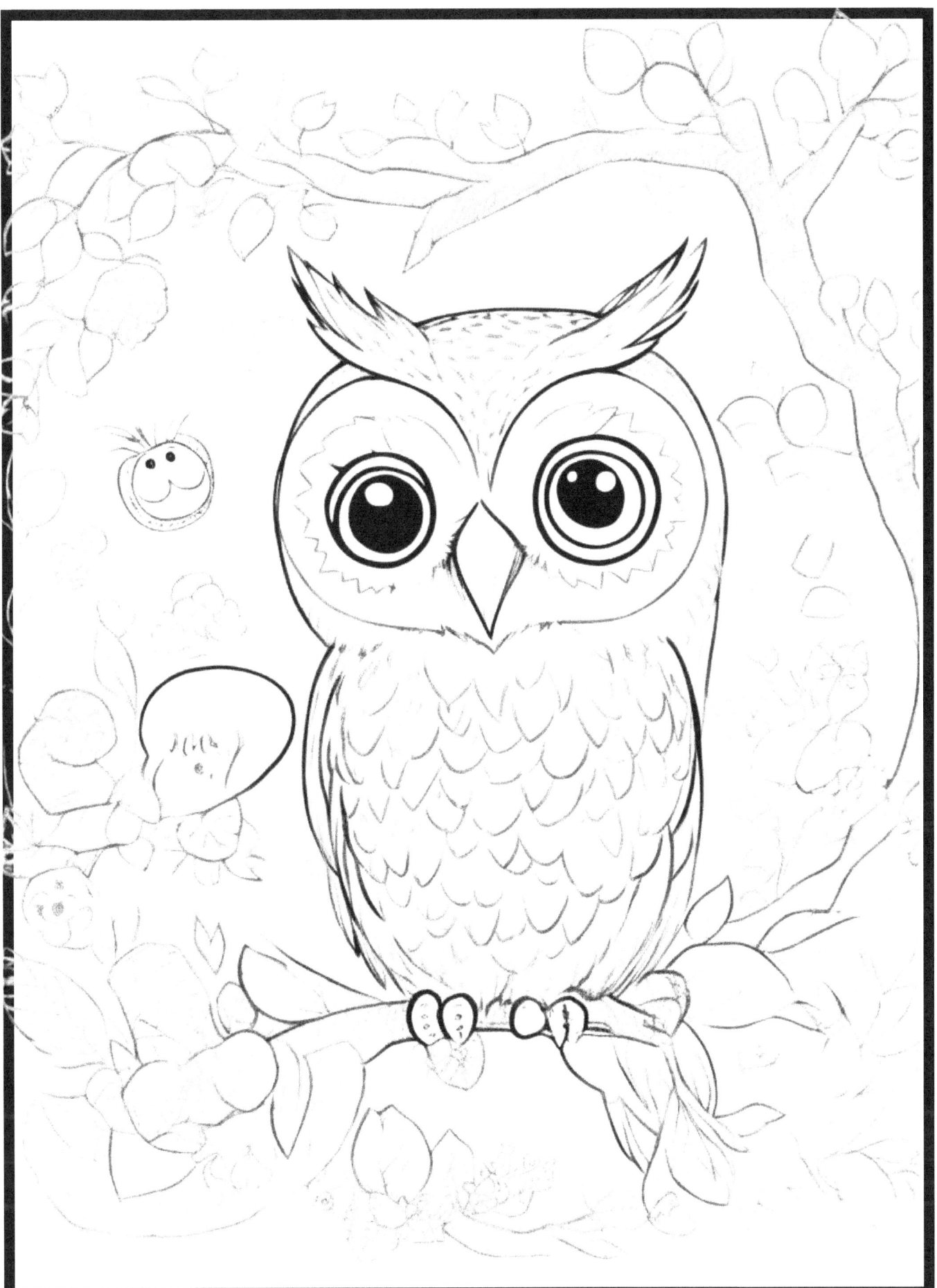

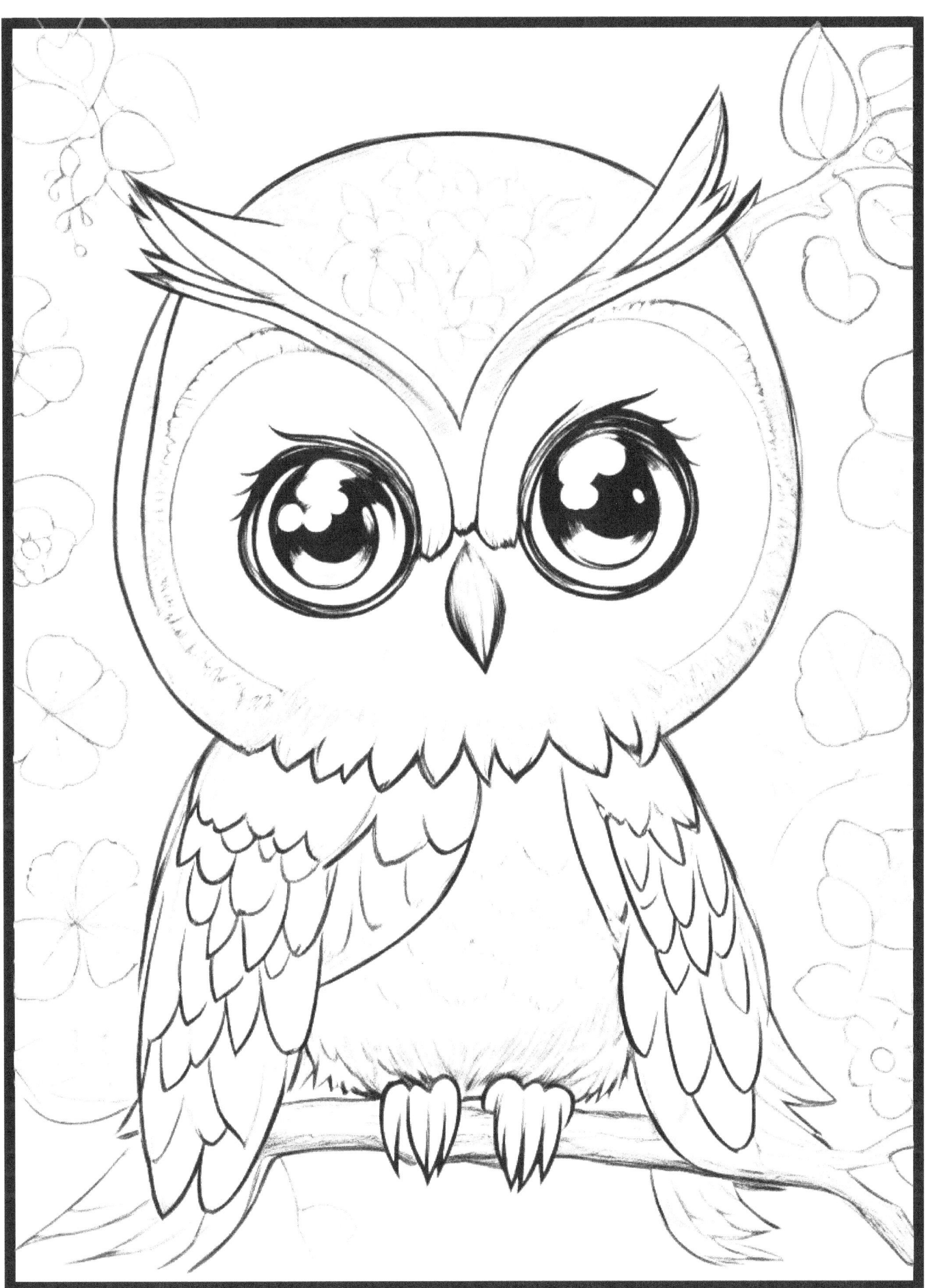

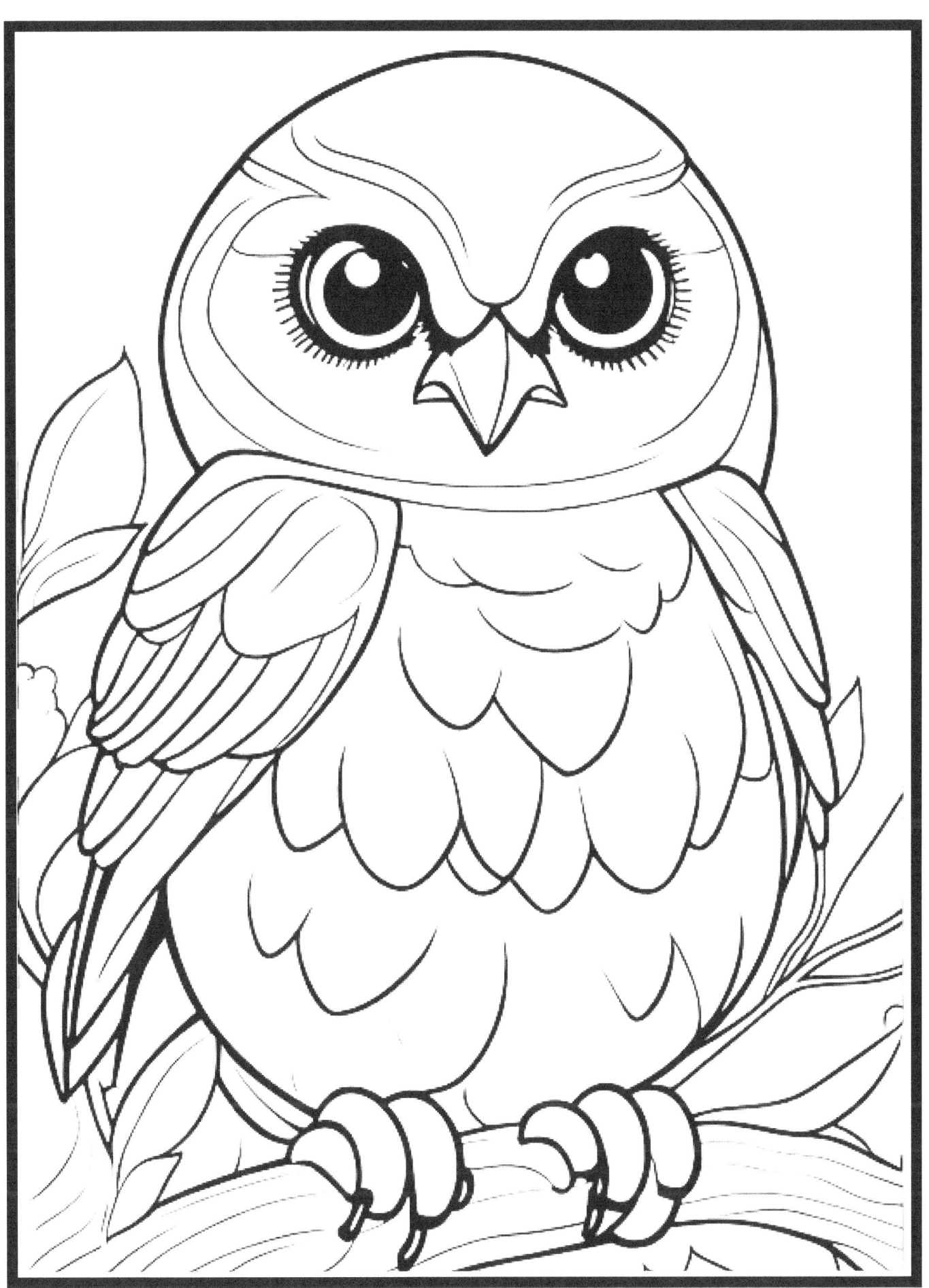

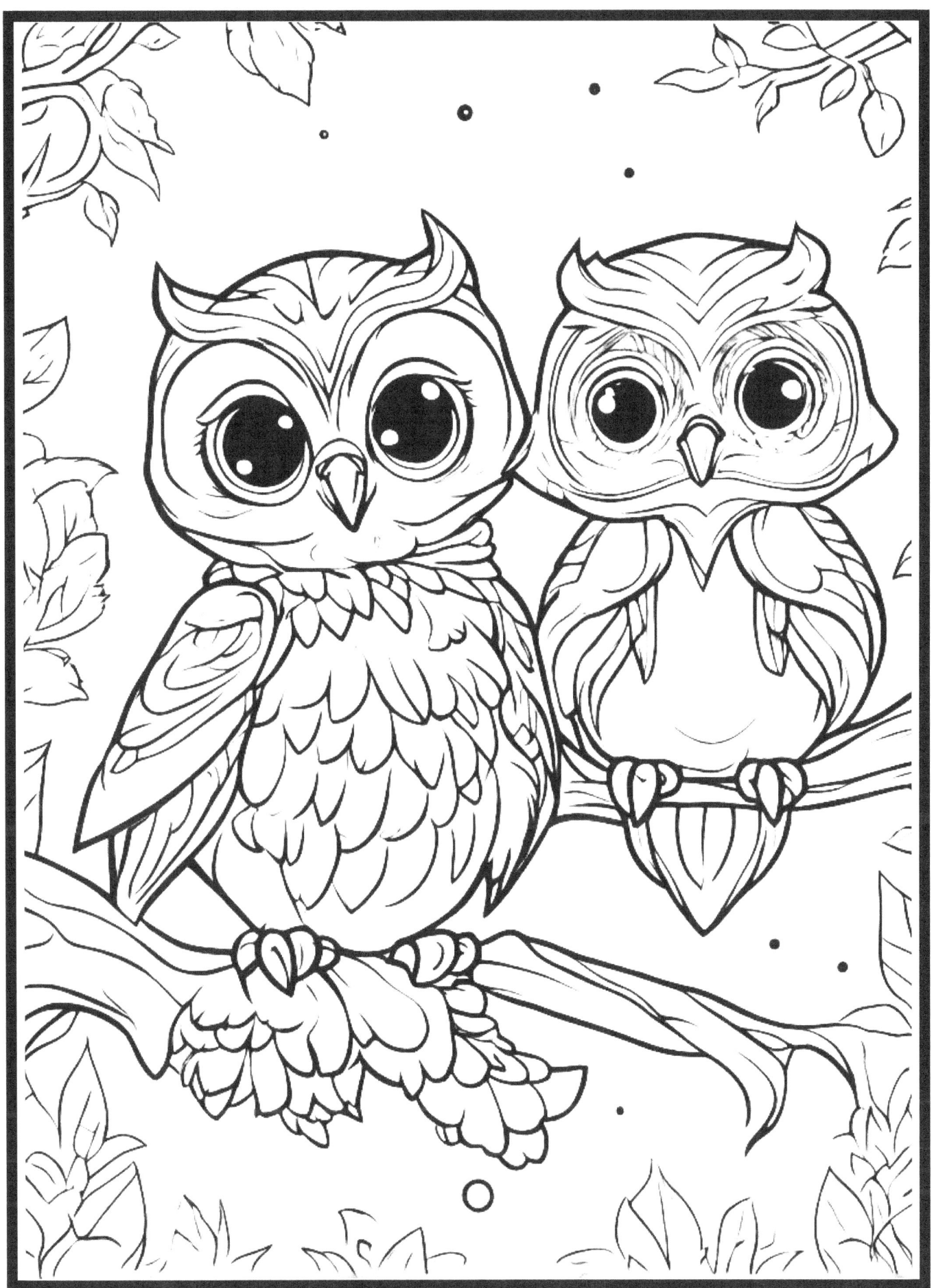

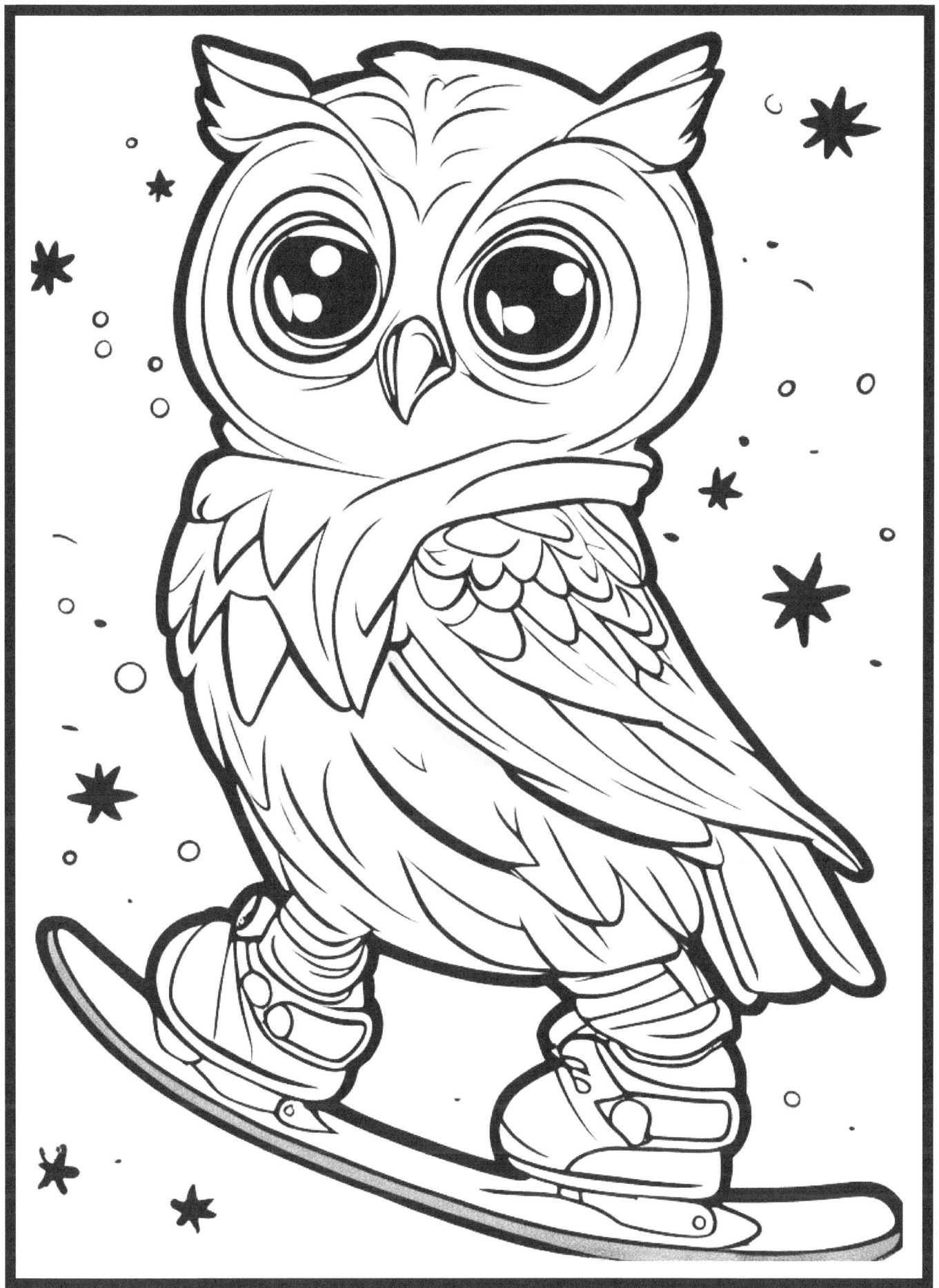

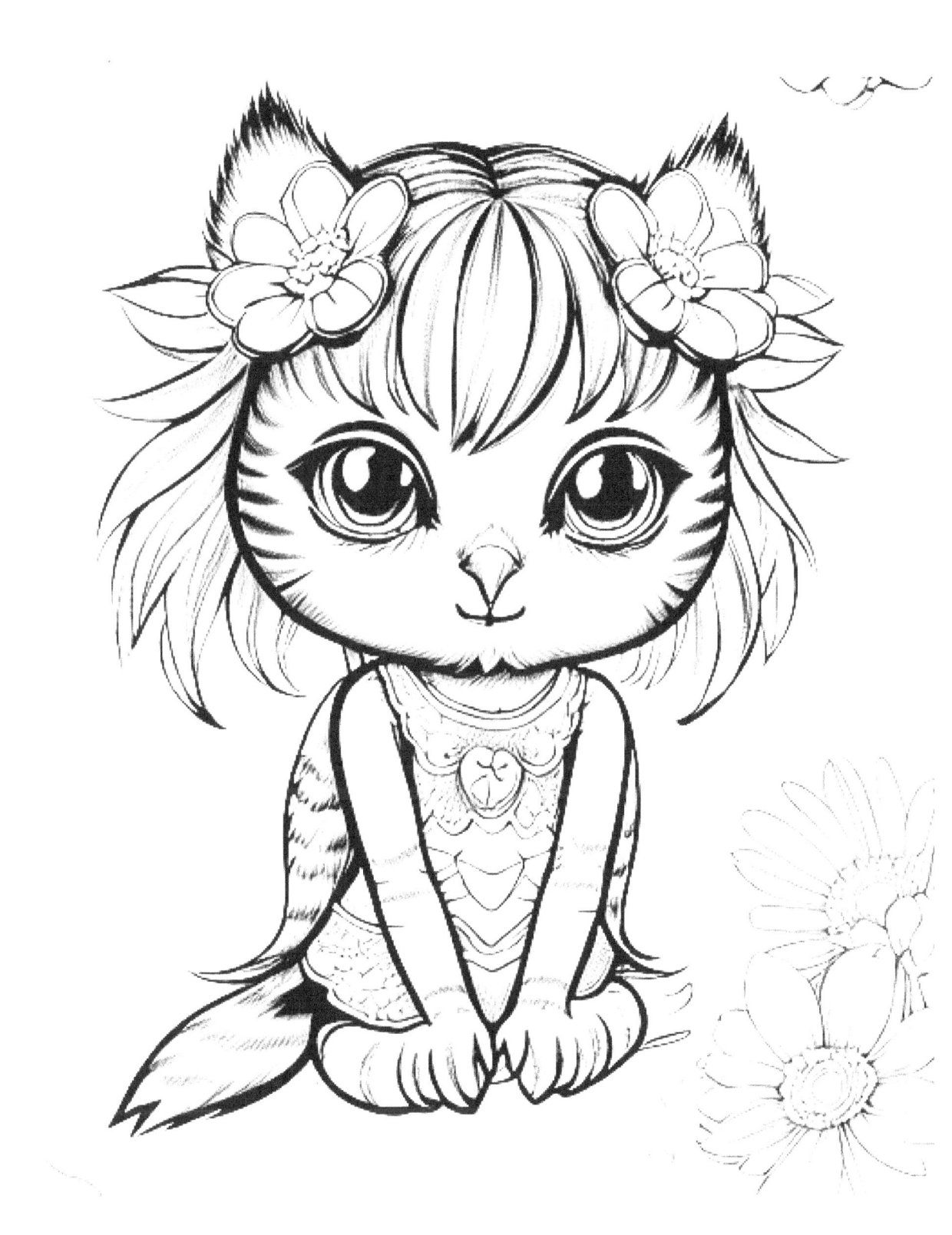

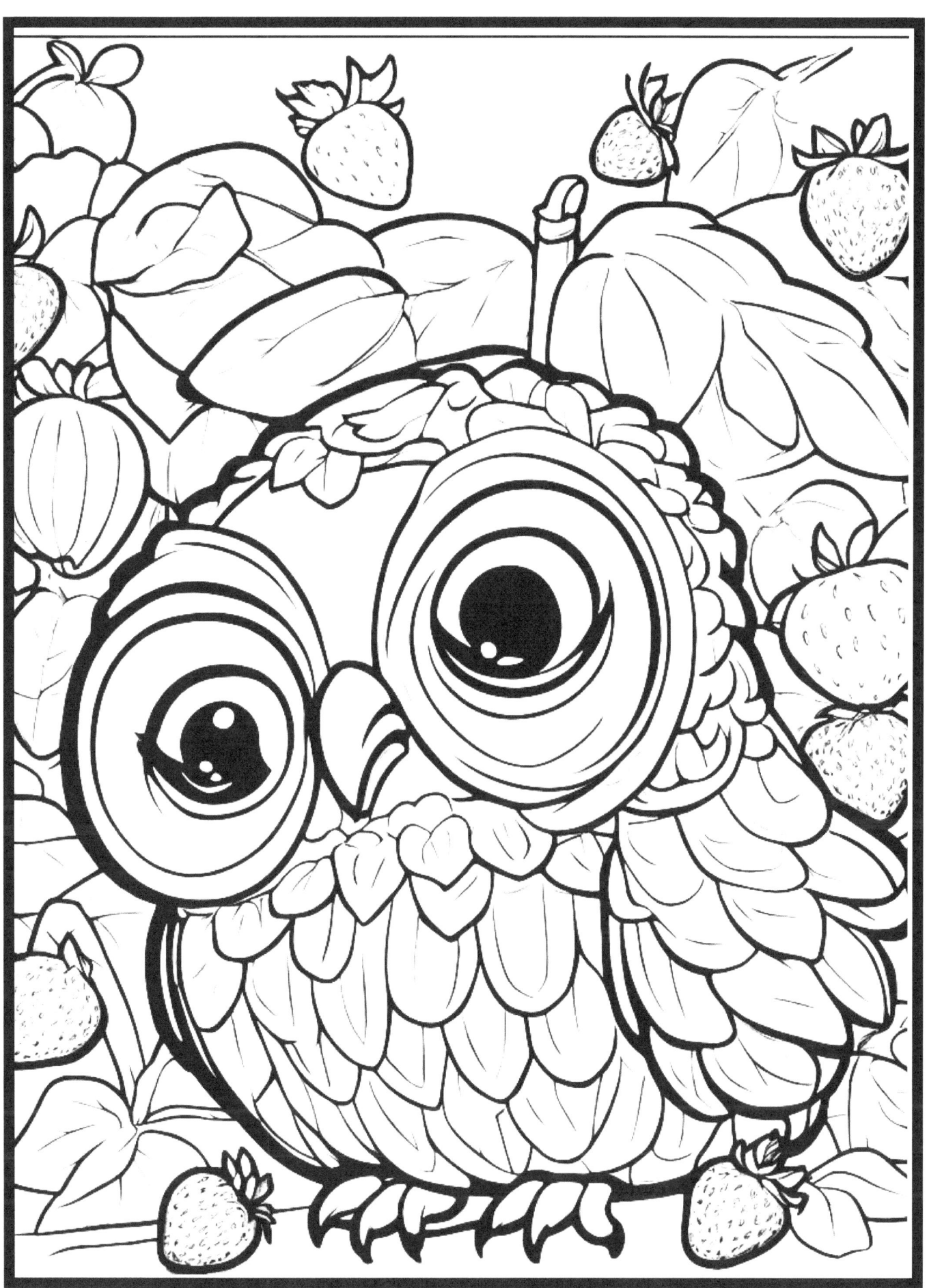

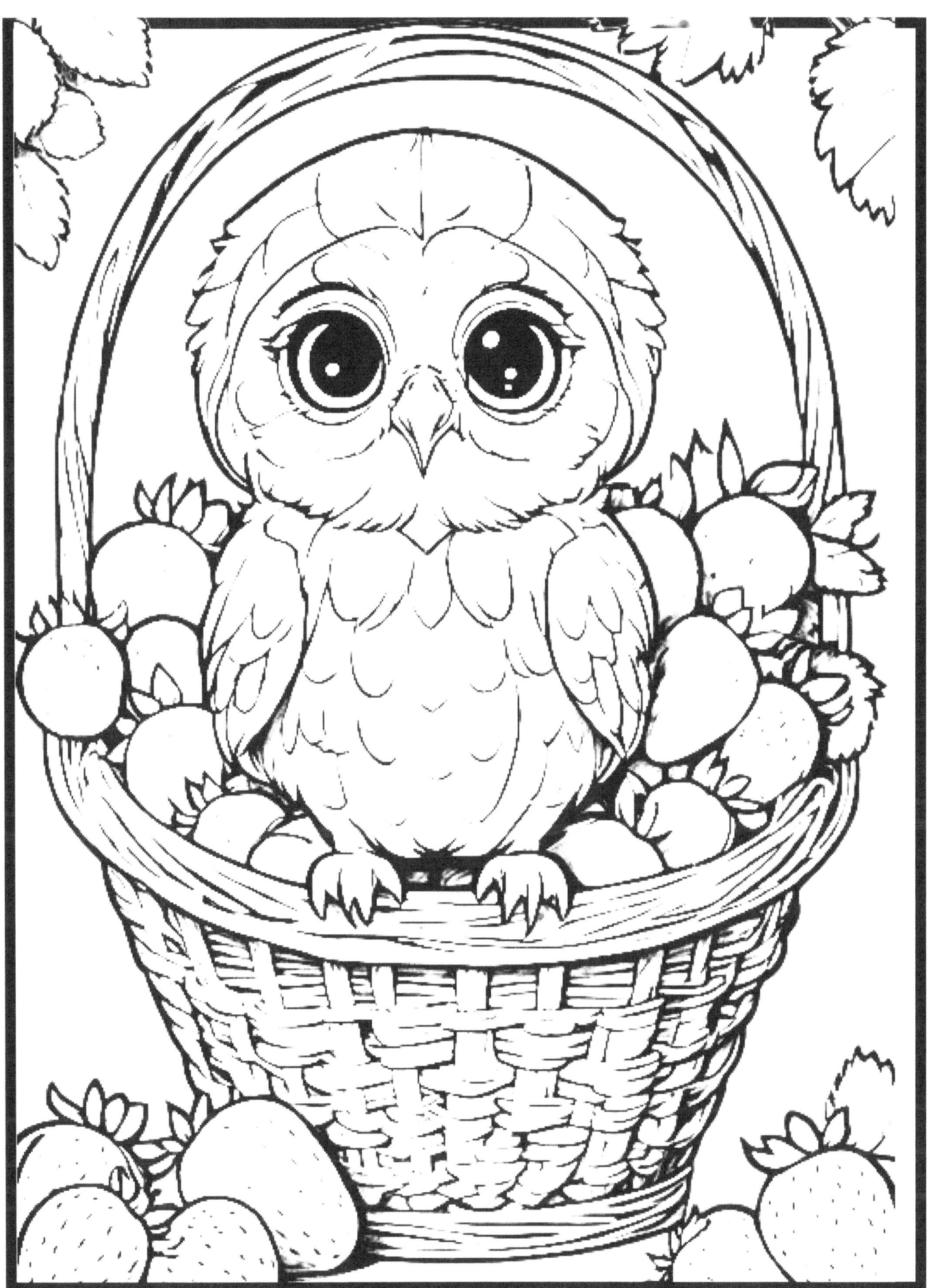

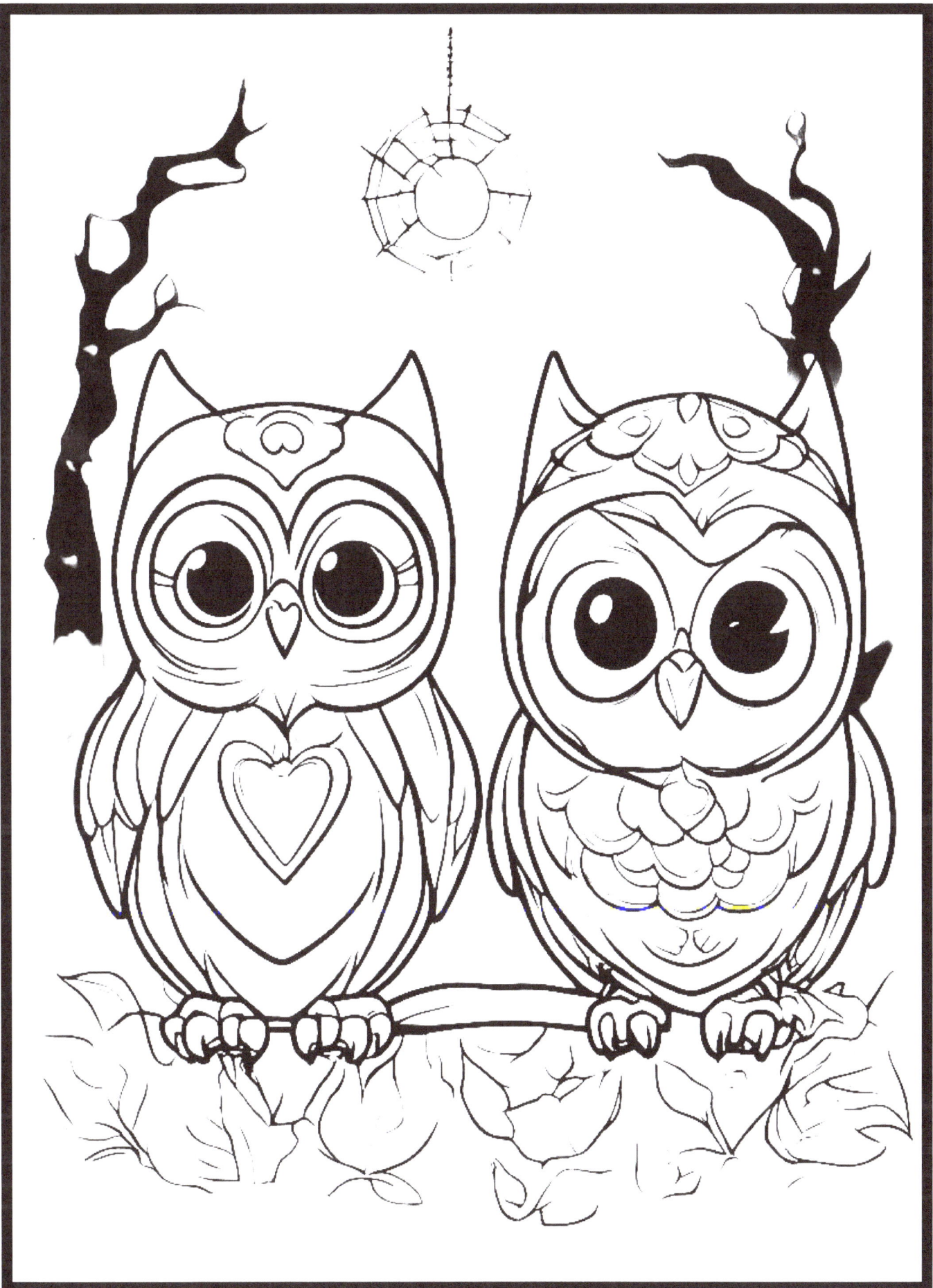

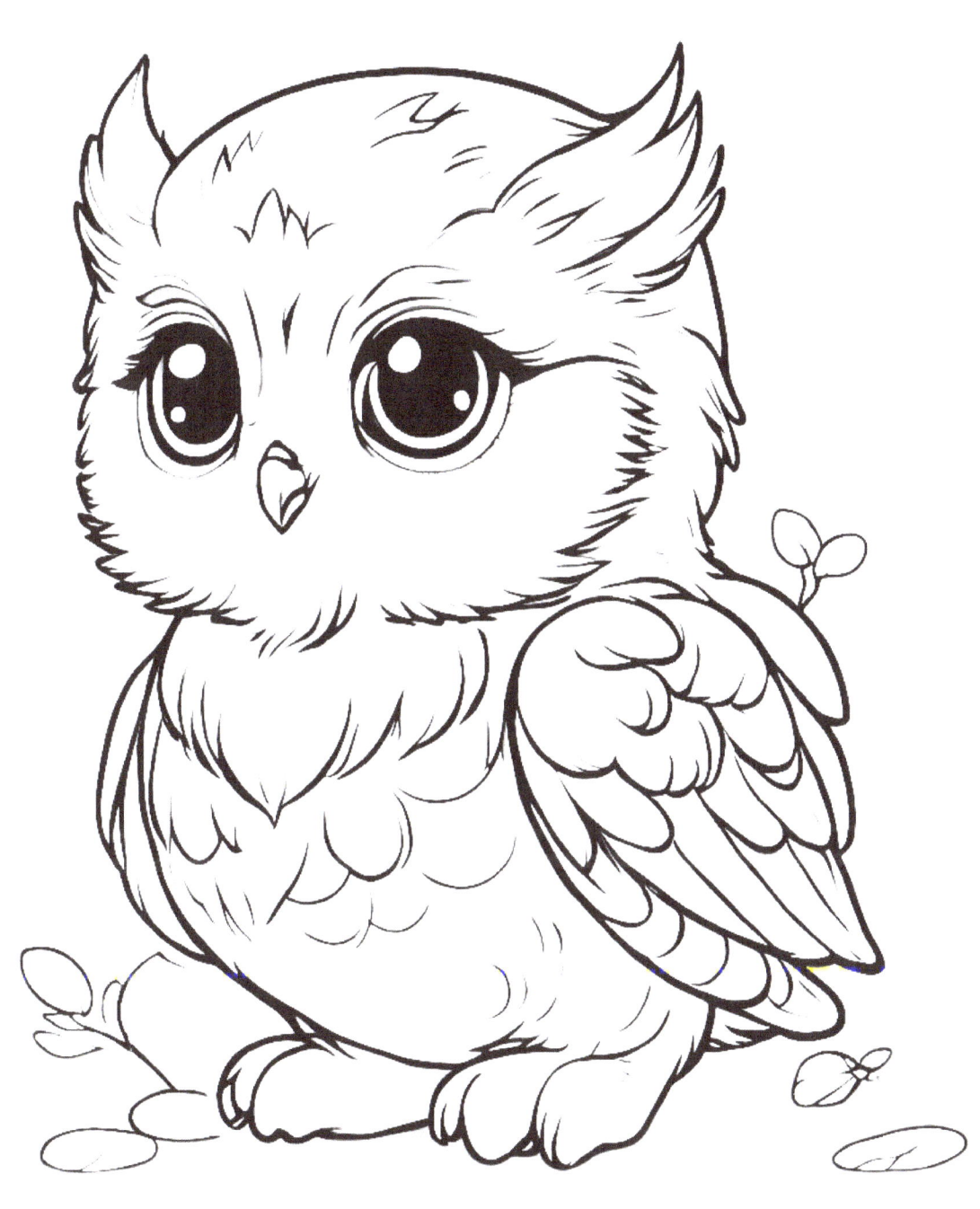

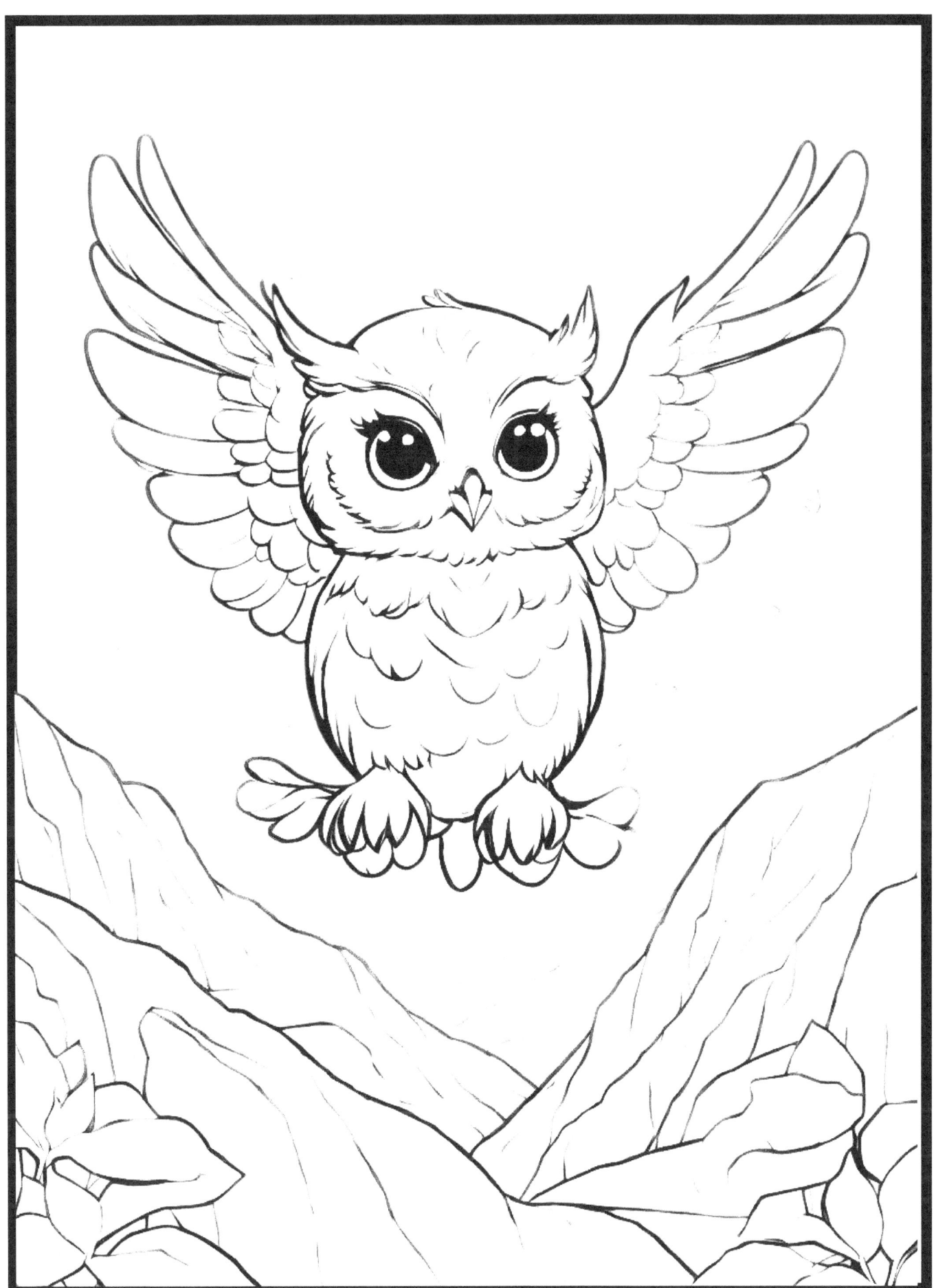

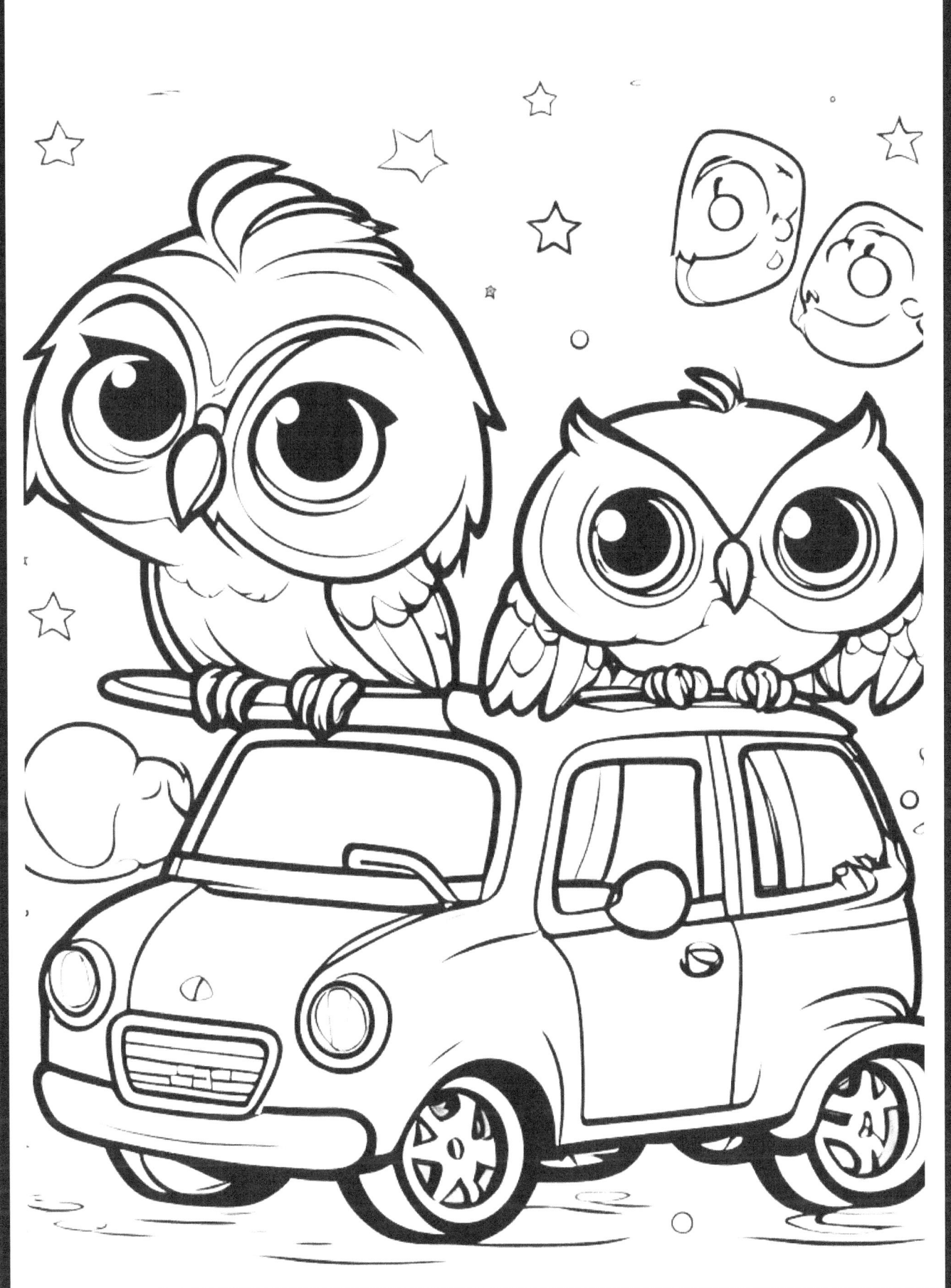

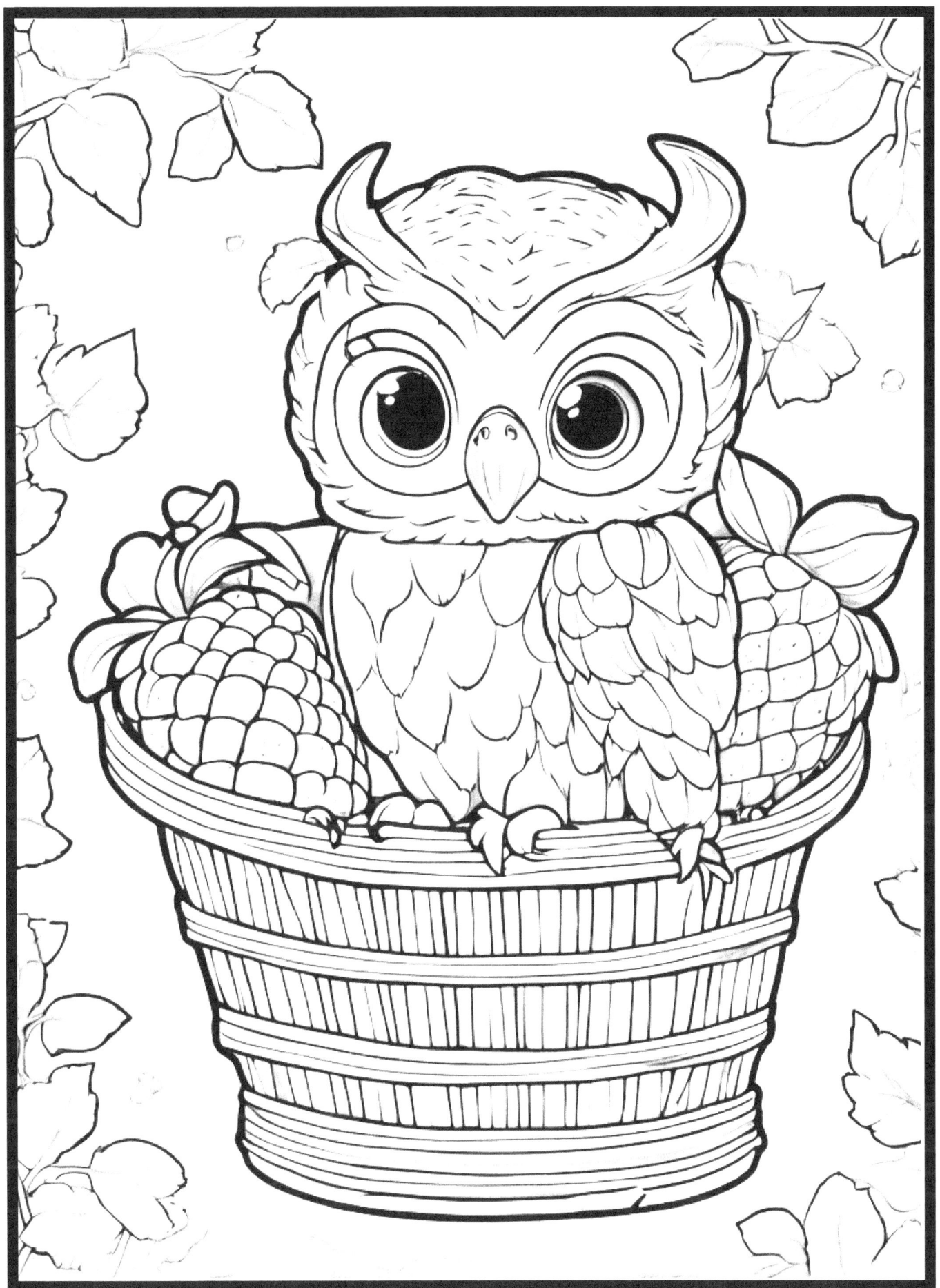

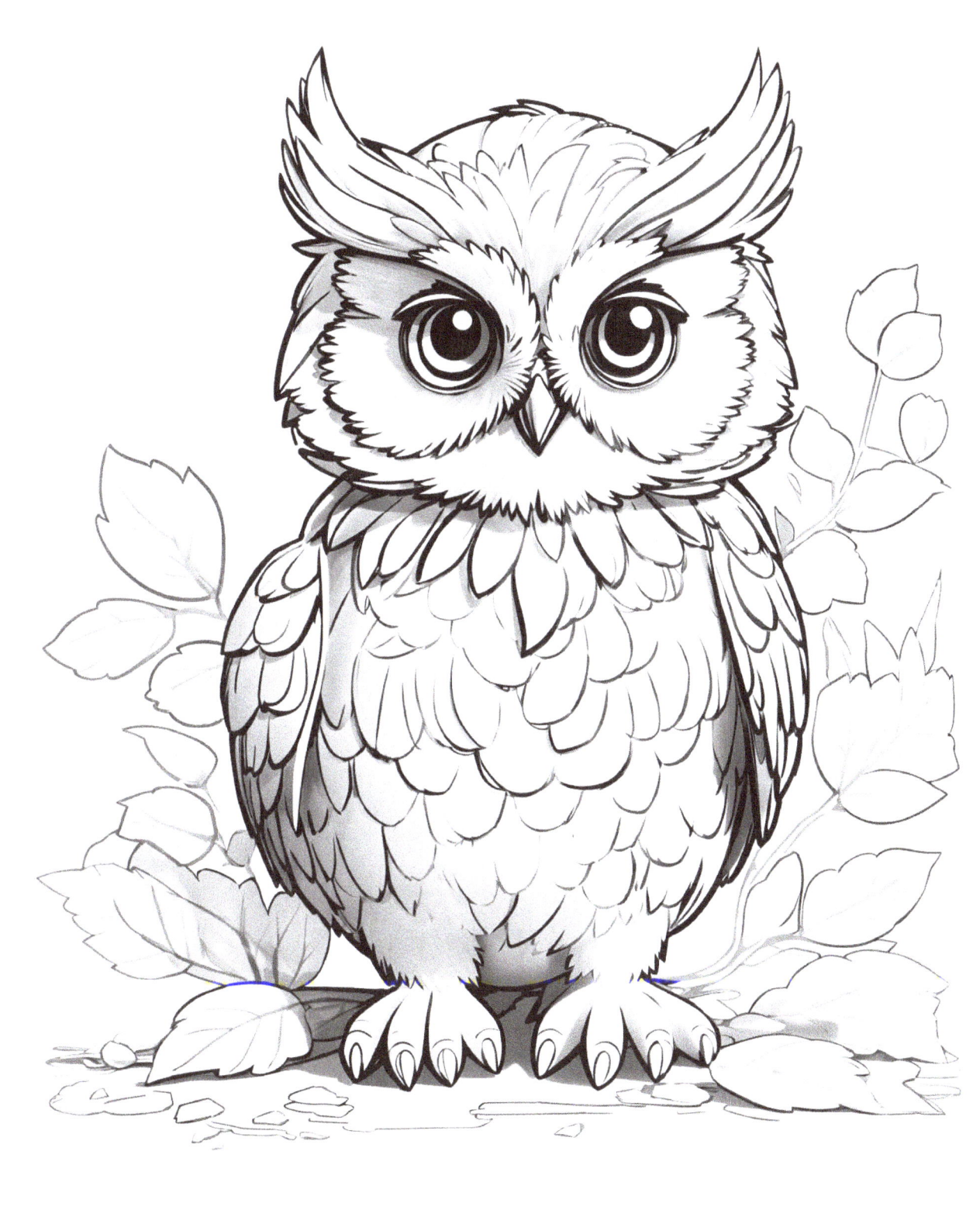

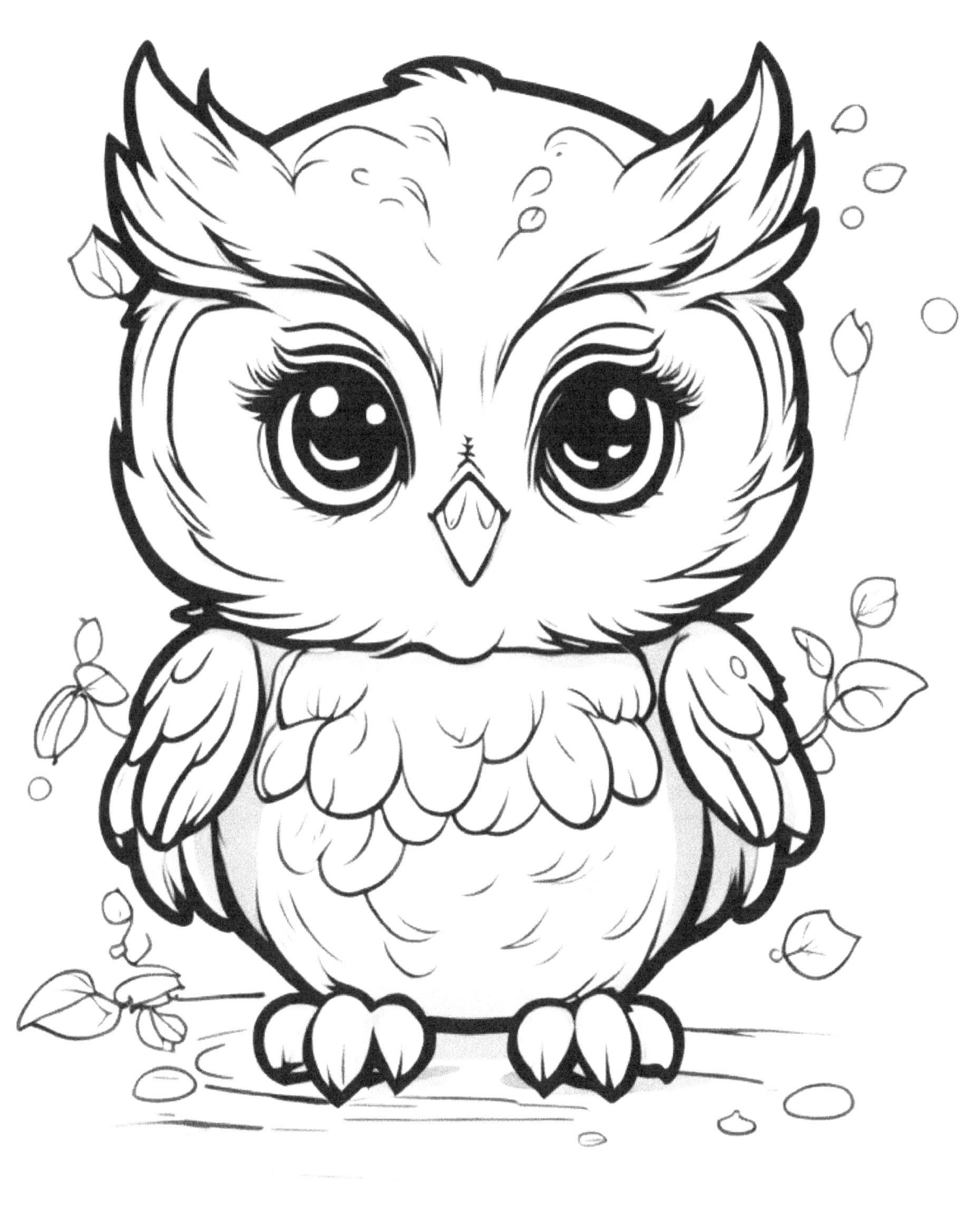

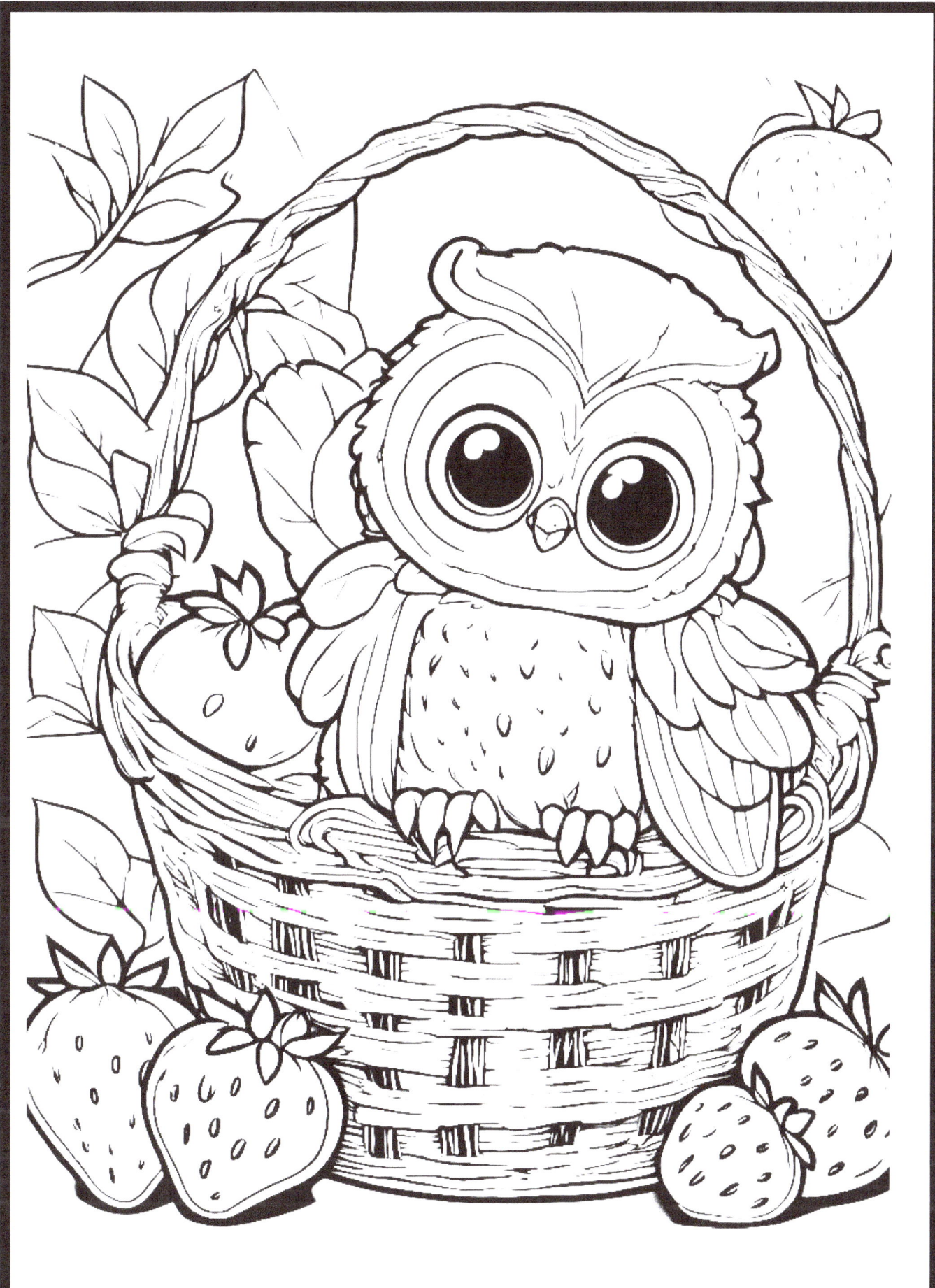

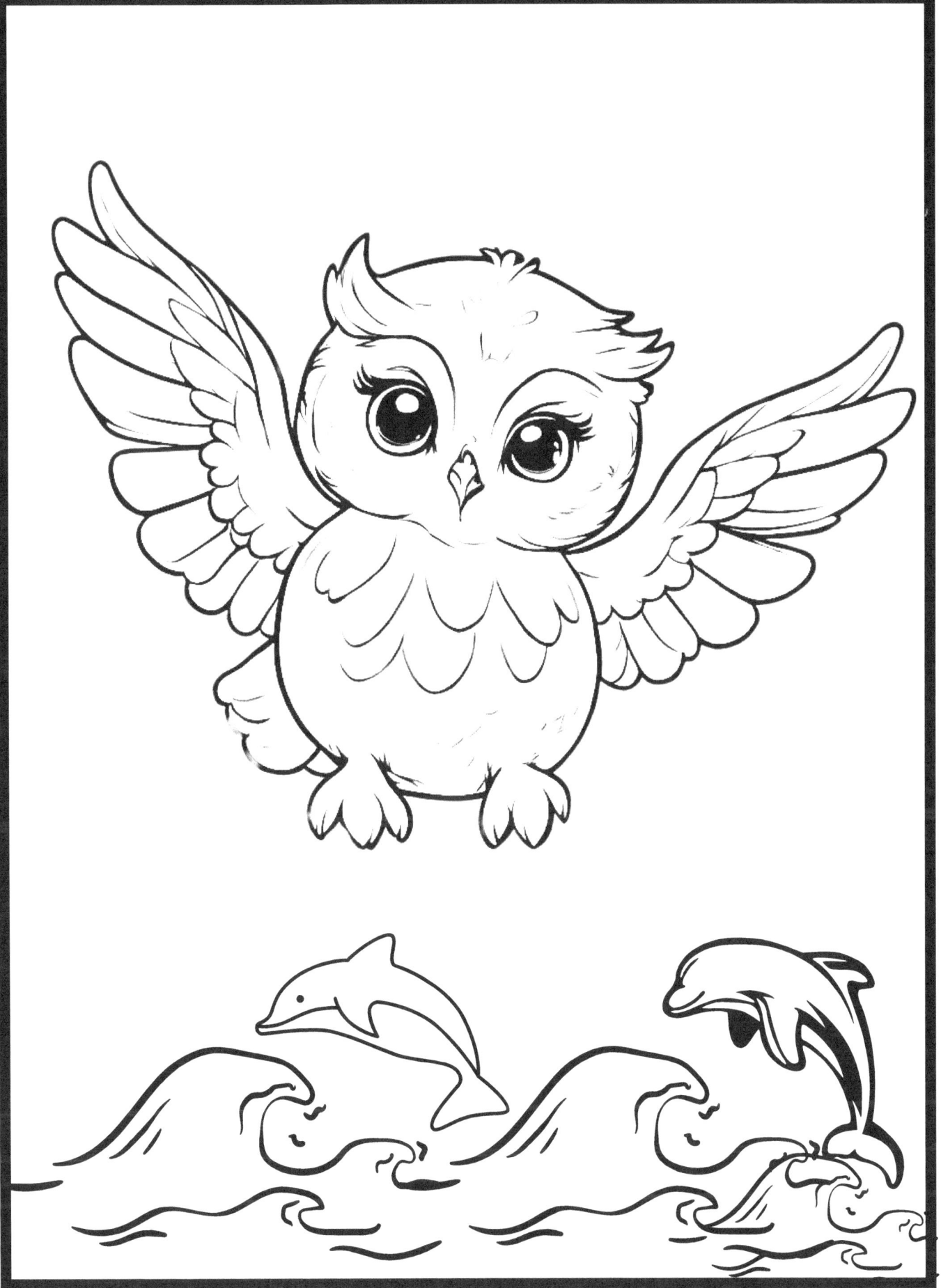

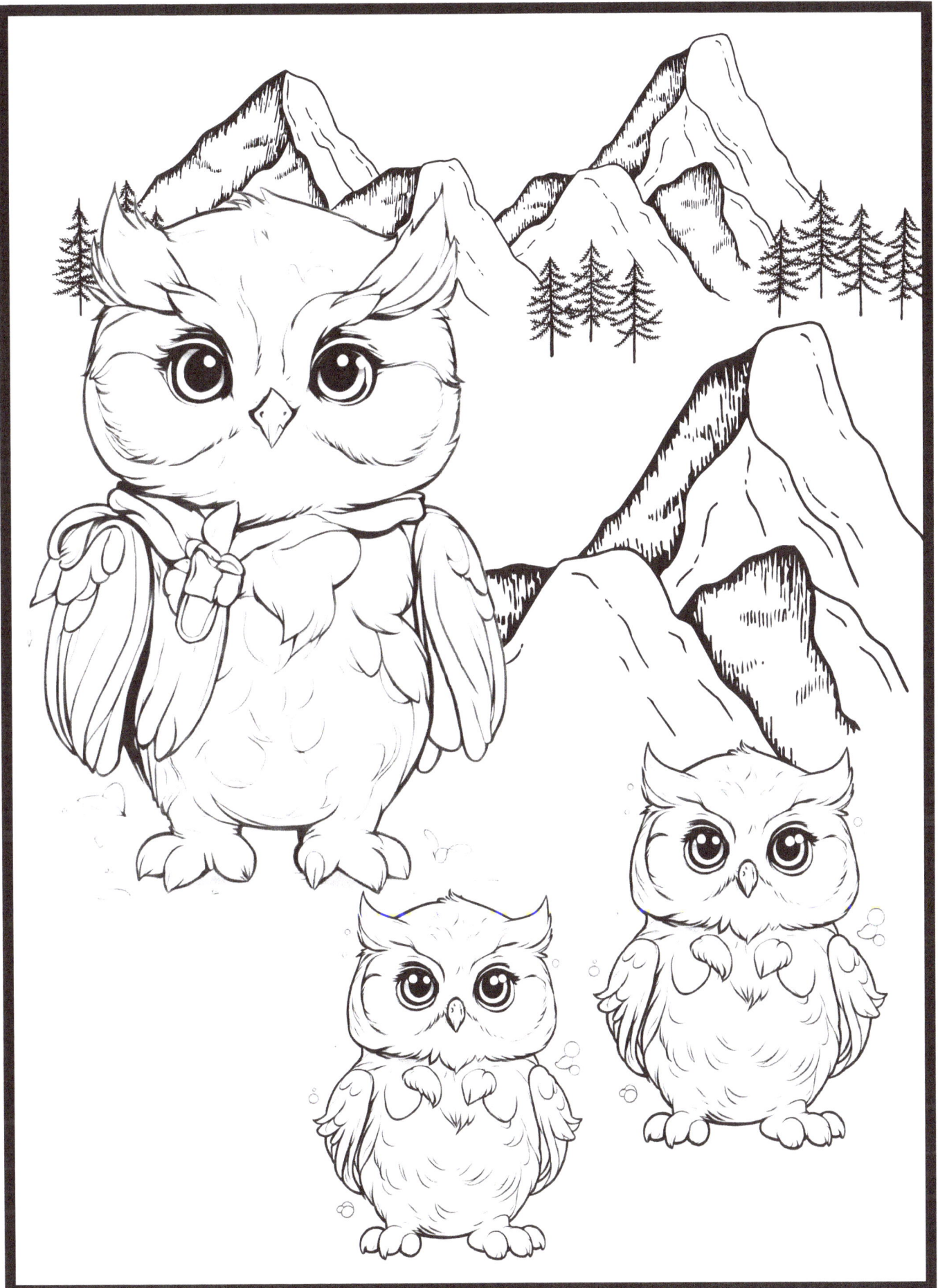

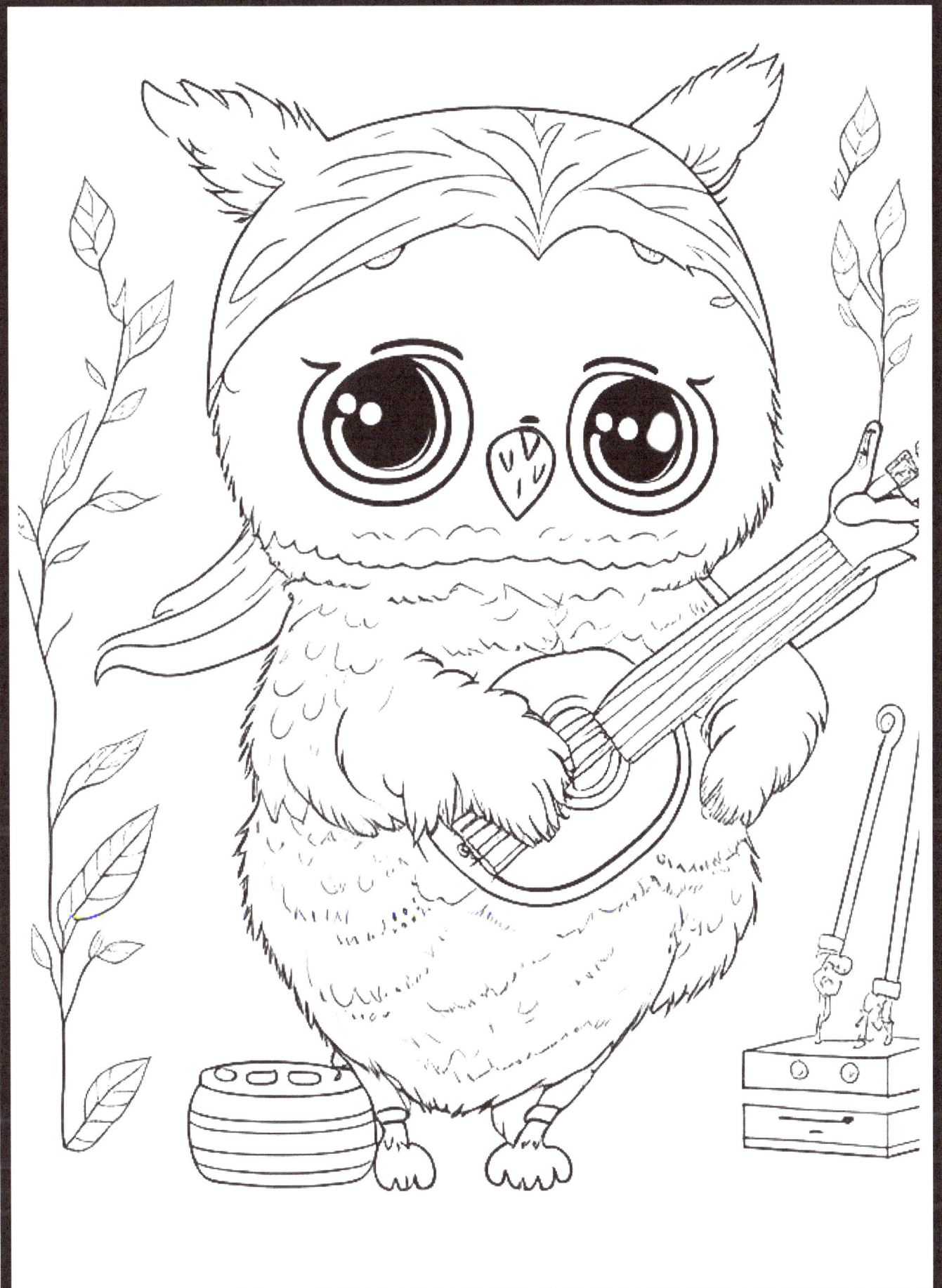

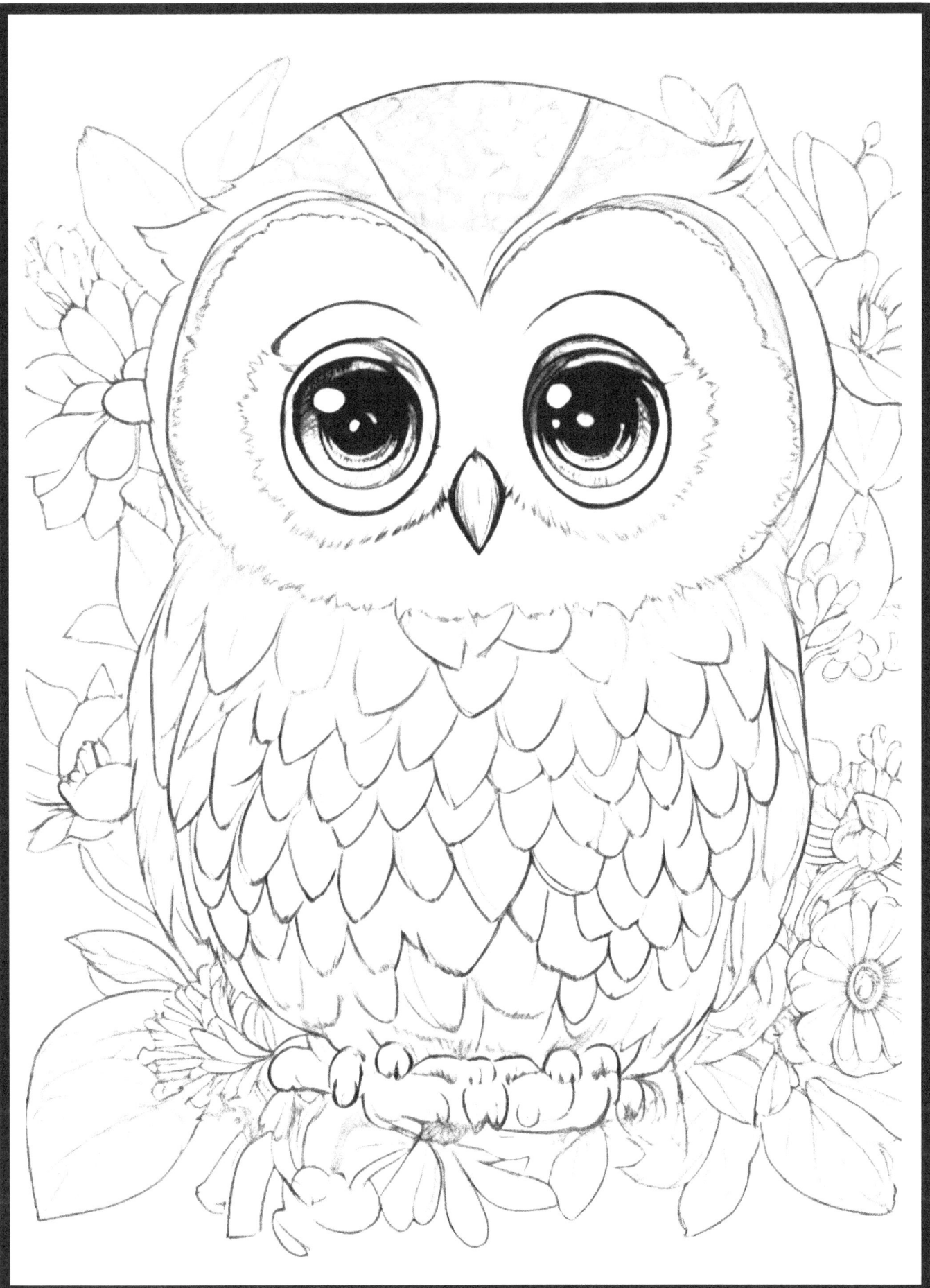

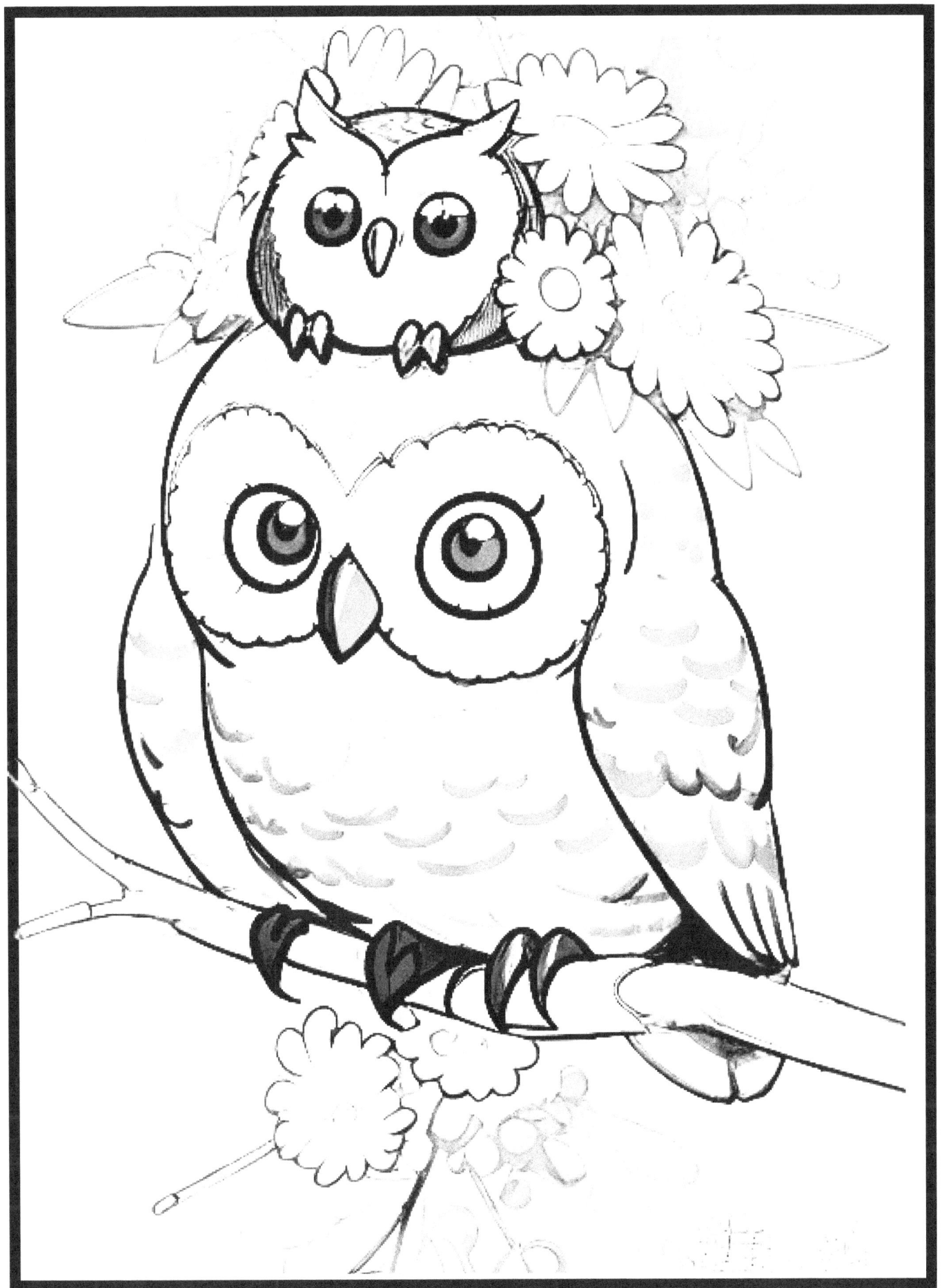

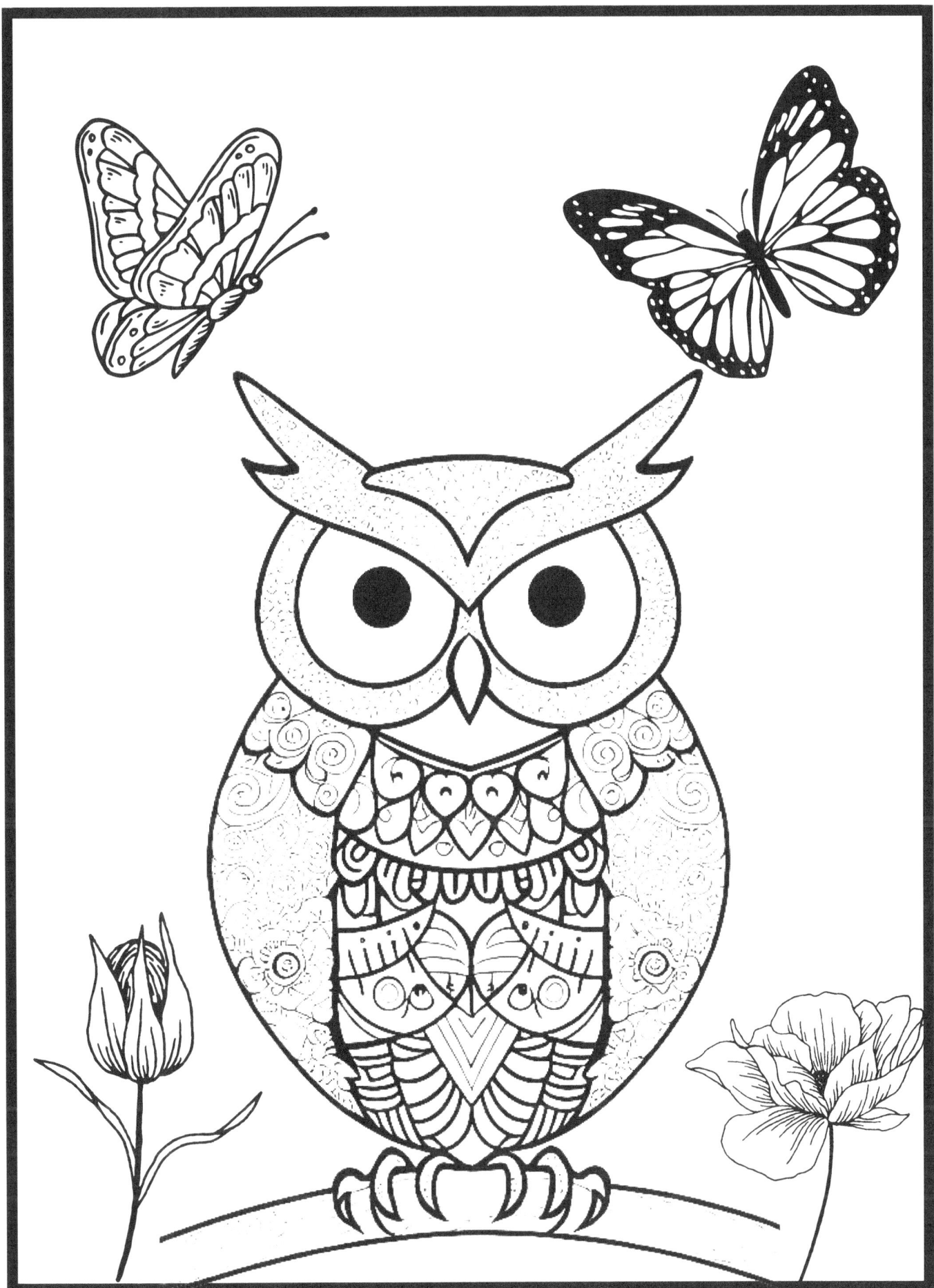

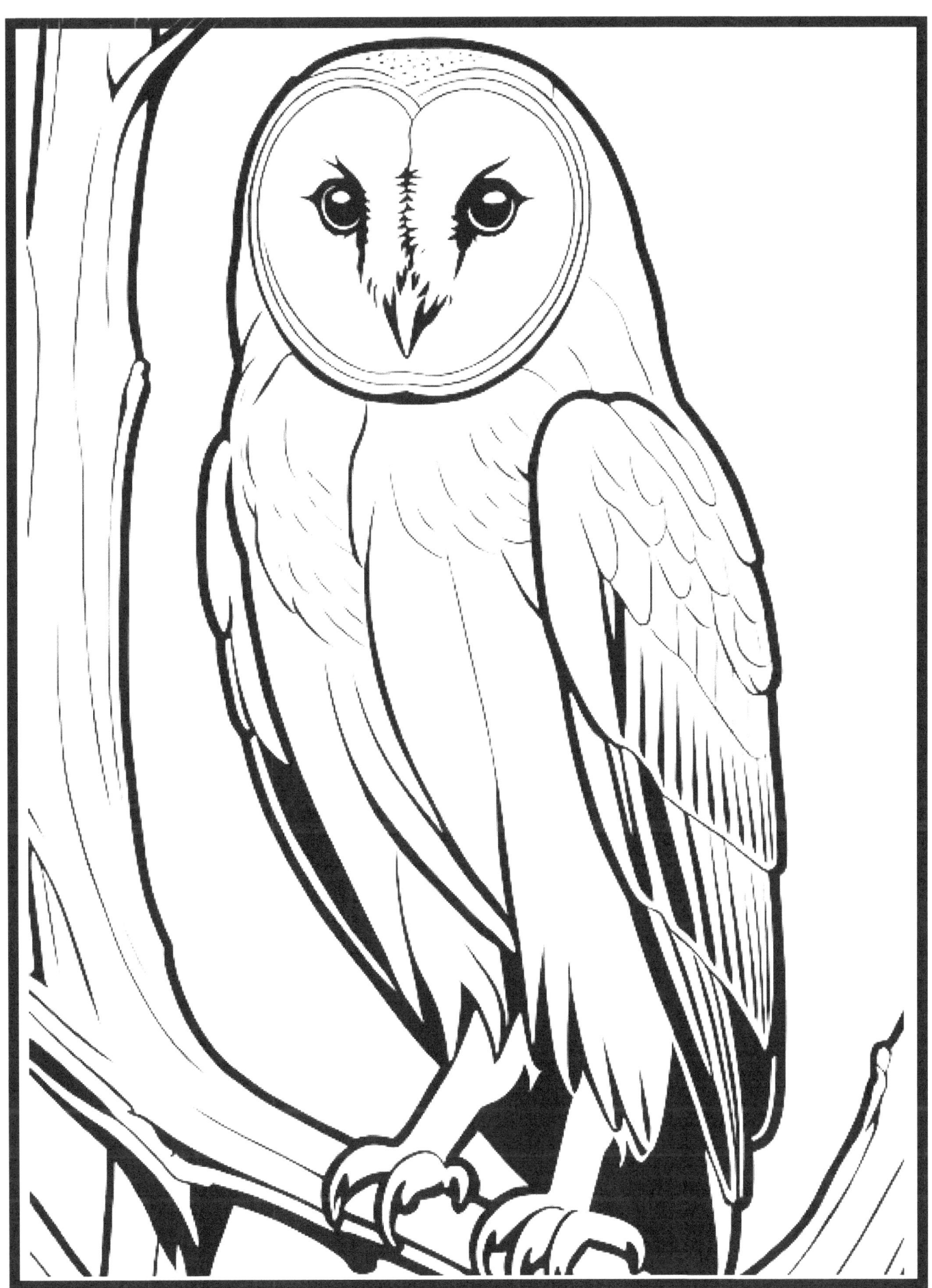

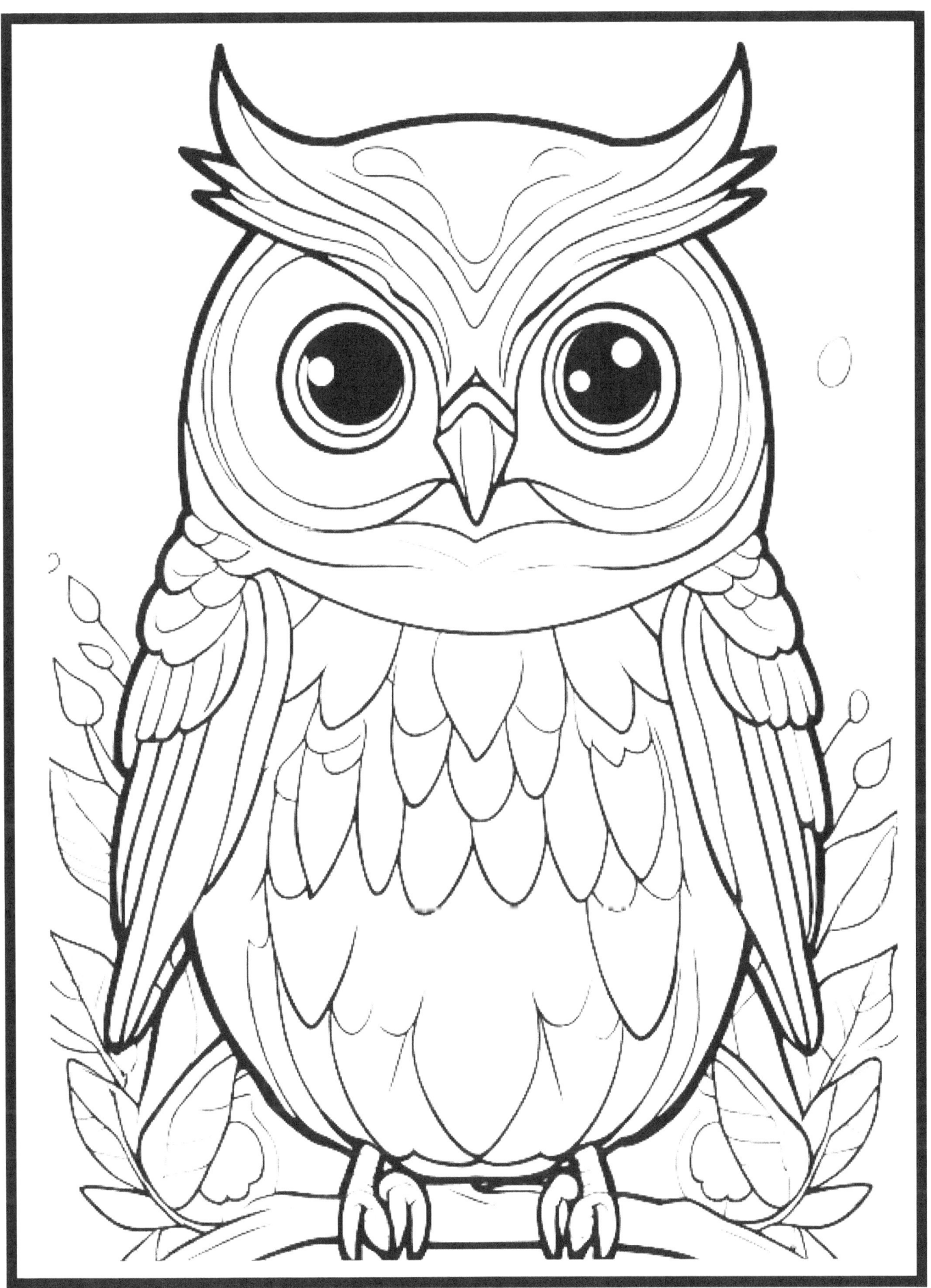

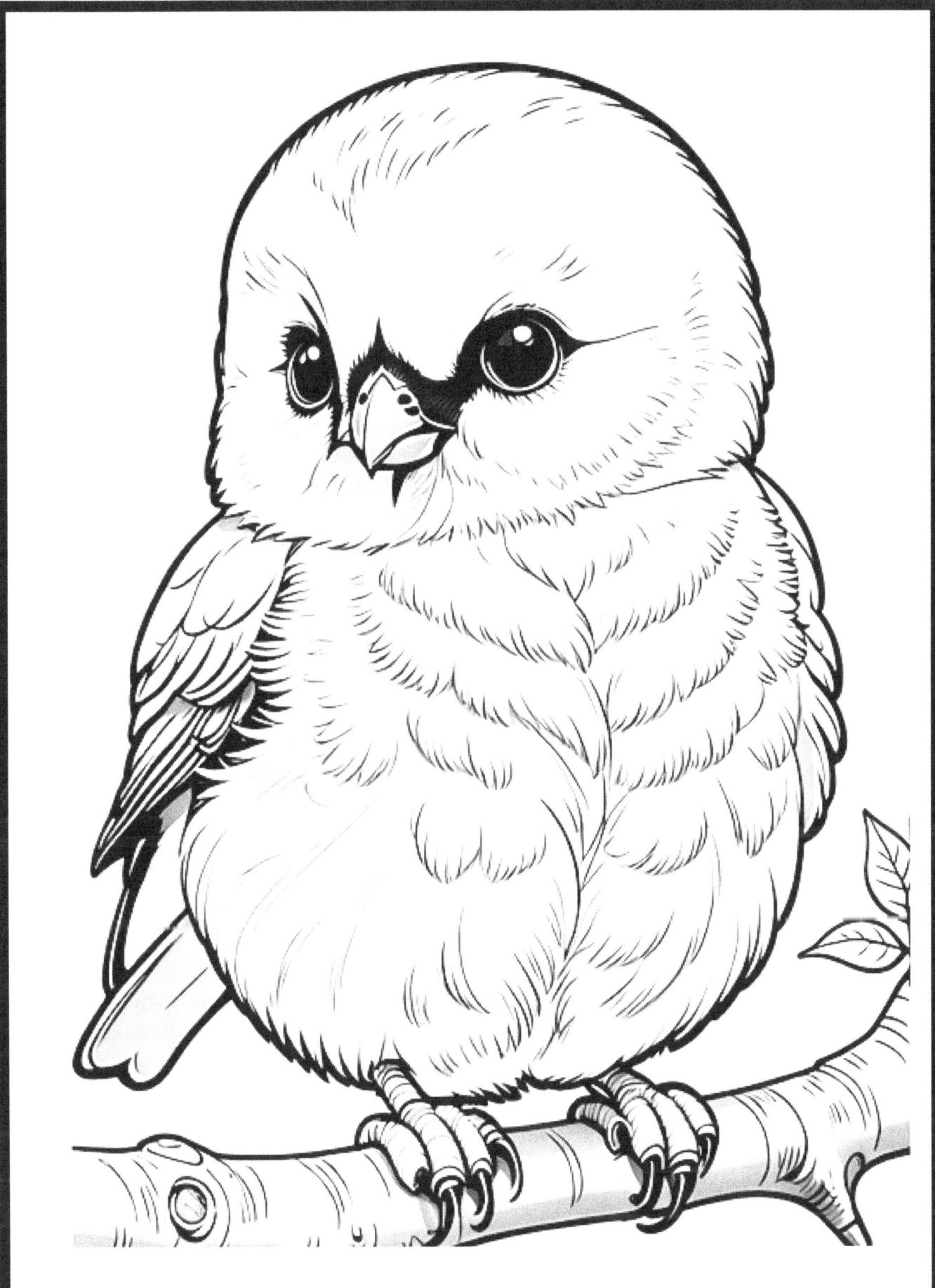

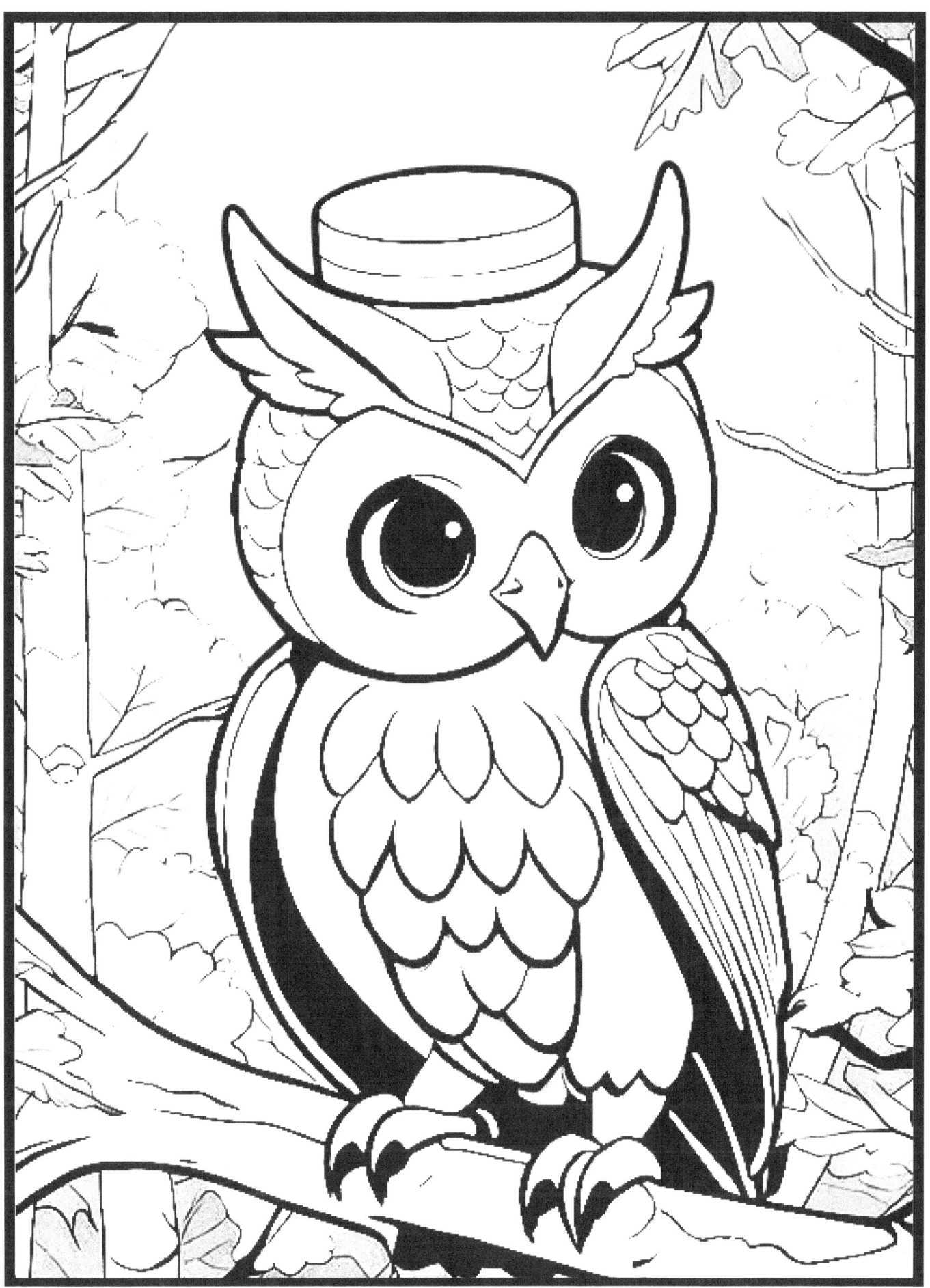